South and Southeast
Wind Atlas

South and Southeast Wind Atlas

Dean DeHarpporte

**State by State Maps
of Wind Speed and Wind Energy**

Missouri	Virginia
Arkansas	North Carolina
Louisiana	Mississippi
Kentucky	Alabama
Tennessee	Georgia
West Virginia	South Carolina
Delaware	Florida
Maryland	

VNR **VAN NOSTRAND REINHOLD COMPANY**
NEW YORK   CINCINNATI   TORONTO   LONDON   MELBOURNE

Copyright © 1984 by Van Nostrand Reinhold Company Inc.

Library of Congress Catalog Card Number: 83-10481
ISBN: 0-442-21822-2

All rights reserved. No part of this work covered by the copyright hereon may be reproduced or used in any form or by any means—graphic, electronic, or mechanical, including photocopying, recording, taping, or information storage and retrieval systems—without permission of the publisher.

Manufactured in the United States of America

Published by Van Nostrand Reinhold Company Inc.
135 West 50th Street
New York, New York 10020

Van Nostrand Reinhold Company Limited
Molly Millars Lane
Wokingham, Berkshire RG11 2PY, England

Van Nostrand Reinhold
480 Latrobe Street
Melbourne, Victoria 3000, Australia

Macmillan of Canada
Division of Gage Publishing Limited
164 Commander Boulevard
Agincourt, Ontario M1S 3C7, Canada

15 14 13 12 11 10 9 8 7 6 5 4 3 2 1

Library of Congress Cataloging in Publication Data

DeHarpporte, Dean.
   South and southeast wind atlas.

   1. Winds — United States — Atlases. I. Title.
QC940.U5D43   1983   515.5'17'0975   83-10481
ISBN 0-442-21822-2

Preface

The *South and Southeast Wind Atlas* is based on research done for the U.S. Department of Energy by Battelle-Pacific Northwest Laboratory in 1980–1981. All maps were reproduced directly from the following publications:

1. Wind Energy Resource Atlas: Volume 7—The South Central Region, PNL-3195 WERA-7, UC-80, prepared by Institute for Storm Research for Pacific Northwest Laboratory, under agreement E-87923-A-L.
2. Wind Energy Resource Atlas: Volume 5—The East Central Region, PNL-3195 WERA-5 UC-60, prepared for the U.S. Department of Energy by NUS Corporation, Rockville, MD, under agreement B-87924-A-L.
3. Wind Energy Resource Atlas: Volume 6—The Southeast Region, PNL-3195 WERA-6, prepared by Geomet Technologies, Inc., Gaithersburg, MD, for Pacific Northwest Laboratory, under agreement 87925-A-L.

The Pacific Northwest Laboratory Atlases have been simplified and interpreted by Dean DeHarpporte, who is a professional meteorologist and a consultant in wind energy research.

Contents

Preface v

1 Introduction 1

    How to Use This Atlas   3
    Variation of Average Wind Speed by Season   2
    Variation of Average Wind Speed by Day and Night   3
    Relationship of Wind Speed and Wind Power   3
    Wind Speed and Wind Power Data   4
    Estimating a Wind Machine's Reduction of Electric Bills   4

2 Southeast Central Region 7

    General Information   7
    Missouri   10
    Arkansas   17
    Louisiana   23
    Wind Speed and Wind Power at Various Locations in the Southeast Central Region   29

3 East Central Region 32

    General Information   32
    Kentucky   35
    Tennessee   42
    West Virginia   49
    Maryland-Delaware   56
    Virginia   63
    North Carolina   70
    Wind Speed and Wind Power at Various Locations in the East Central Region   77

4 Southeast Region 80

    General Information   80
    Mississippi   83
    Alabama   89
    Georgia   96
    South Carolina   103
    Florida   110
    Wind Speed and Wind Power at Various Locations in the Southeast Region   117

South and Southeast
Wind Atlas

1
Introduction

This Wind Speed Atlas contains detailed maps of average wind speed for each state in the Southeast Central Region (Missouri, Arkansas, and Louisiana), each state in the East Central Region (Kentucky, Tennessee, West Virginia, Delaware, Maryland, Virginia, and North Carolina), and each state in the Southeast (Mississippi, Alabama, Georgia, South Carolina, and Florida). To determine the average wind speed in your area, simply find your location on your state map. Other maps and graphs for your state show how wind speed varies through the cycle of the seasons and between day and night.

HOW TO USE THIS ATLAS

If the wind speed (averaged over the whole year) is less than 10 mph at your location, a wind machine will probably produce very little power and may never pay for itself. If your average wind speed is near or above 12 mph, however, you are located in a region where winds blow at a speed that most wind machines are designed for. In this location, a wind machine will provide adequate power and may pay for itself within a number of years. Areas where the average wind speed is above 15 mph are rare, but in those areas (some ridge tops, shore areas, and islands) electricity produced by wind power will be among the cheapest methods of producing power.

This Atlas describes average wind speed in terms of wind speed classes: the lowest, Class 1, has the lowest wind speeds, and the highest, Class 7, has the highest. In most areas of each state shown on the maps to be Class 1, the average wind speed is less than 10 mph. Most Class 7 areas, on the other hand, have average wind speeds of more than 16 mph. Between Class 1 and Class 7, the average wind speed is between about 10 and 16 mph, as shown in the table at the top of the following page.*

Areas where the wind speed class is 6 or 7 are obviously the best locations for wind machines. Areas designated Class 3, 4, or 5 are good potential wind machine sites, whereas Class 2 areas are marginal. Most Class 1 areas are not suitable for wind machines; however, some Class 1 areas that are best exposed to the wind (on hilltops, for example) may have adequate wind speeds for wind machine operation.

AVERAGE YEARLY WIND SPEED (mph)	CORRESPONDING WIND SPEED CLASS
Below 9.8	1
9.8–11.5	2
11.6–12.5	3
12.6–13.4	4
13.5–14.3	5
14.4–15.7	6
Above 15.7	7

The higher above ground a wind machine is installed, the stronger the wind speed. Wind speed increases about 1 mph for each 35-ft increase in height. Wind speeds are always higher on high ground or hilltops than in areas sheltered from the free flow of the wind.

In many of the maps included in this Atlas, mountainous areas are shaded gray. In these shaded areas, the wind class shown applies only to the exposed parts of the mountains. The exposed parts are ridges or crests, peaks, and, in some cases, passes. The valleys between the mountains and the lower portions of the slopes usually have low average wind speeds, ordinarily unsuitable for wind machines. When considering the siting of a wind machine in a valley, keep in mind that if the valley is located on a portion of a map shaded gray, the wind speed class indicated does not apply to the lower portions of the valley. Rather, the wind speed class in the valley is not shown but is probably substantially lower than the wind speed class that applies to the surrounding mountain summits.

Although this Atlas contains the newest and most accurate information on wind speeds available, there are undoubtedly borderline or remote areas where the actual wind speed varies by one or more classes from the class shown here. The only way to be positive that wind speeds are high enough (or too low) for the use of a wind machine at your location is to measure the wind speed for at least three months, and preferably for a whole year.

VARIATION OF AVERAGE WIND SPEED BY SEASON

The variation of wind speed by season is an important consideration in choosing a wind machine. In the South Central, East Central, and Southeast regions, wind speeds are usually strongest in winter and spring. The most appropriate use for a wind machine might therefore be to provide electricity for heating. Wind speeds are usually weakest in summer. A wind machine used for air conditioning might therefore be a poor choice for these states. Of course, if a wind ma-

---

*The relationship between wind speed class and the ranges of wind speed shown in the table are only approximate. The average wind speed at a particular location within a particular wind speed class may be slightly higher or lower than indicated by the table. This is true because the wind speed classes are actually defined by average wind power. For an explanation of the relationship between wind speed and wind power, refer to page 3.

chine is to be used only for the generation of electricity that will be independent of the electric utility, the wind machine will need to be large enough to generate sufficient power during the summer when speeds are usually lowest.

An option would be to choose a wind machine sufficiently large to produce enough electricity for only part of the time during the season of lowest wind speed and to rely on utility power when winds are calm or an unusually large amount of electricity is needed. If this option is chosen, there may be more than enough electricity generated by the wind machine during the season when winds are strongest. In this case, electricity will flow away from the wind machine into the electric utility wires, where it will be routed to other utility customers. The utility is obligated by Federal law to pay the wind machine owner a fair price for this electricity.

If complete independence from the local electric utility is desired, wind-machine-generated electricity may be stored in batteries. When winds are low or calm, the stored electricity can then be used as needed. The disadvantage of this option is the loss of about 25 percent of the electricity in the process of storing it and the high cost of the many batteries needed to store sufficient electricity to tide you over periods of light winds.

Some wind machines are made to produce heat rather than electricity. These wind machines, of course, are designed to take advantage of the strong winds of winter that blow over much of the three regions.

VARIATION OF AVERAGE WIND SPEED BY DAY AND NIGHT

The change of wind speed with the hour of the day may affect your choice of wind machine. Usually, wind speeds are strongest during early afternoon and weakest at night. A wind machine might therefore provide enough electricity to run appliances during the day, but less than enough for lighting purposes at night. To accommodate the differences in the amount of electricity generated, wind machine owners may choose to use electricity from the local utility or electricity stored in batteries.

Winds in the South Central, East Central and Southeast Regions are as much as 100 percent stronger during the afternoon than at dawn and most of the night. The greatest day-night variation occurs during spring and summer; the least, during winter. On mountain ridges, there is only a small variation of wind speed from night to day. In some elevated mountain areas, winds may even be stronger during the night than during the day.

RELATIONSHIP OF WIND SPEED AND WIND POWER

The force of wind on a wind machine blade is proportional to the density of the air and the cube of the wind speed. Measurement of the wind energy available to turn the machine is accomplished by multiplying the air density by the cube of the wind speed. *Half* the air density multiplied by the cube of the wind speed is called the *wind power*. Wind power is the true measure of the force on a wind machine blade and is a better indicator of the amount of energy a wind machine may generate than wind speed itself.

Wind power is measured in units of watts per square meter. Unfamiliarity with this measurement should not be important because it is only necessary to compare wind power (as an alternative to comparing wind speed) between potential wind machine sites.

The wind speed classes used in this Atlas are actually defined by wind power values. The relationship between wind power and wind speed class is shown in the following table:

WIND SPEED CLASS	WIND POWER (WATTS PER SQ. METER)
1	Below 100
2	100–150
3	150–200
4	200–250
5	250–300
6	300–400
7	400–1000

WIND SPEED AND WIND POWER DATA

At the conclusion of Sections 2, 3, and 4, there are tables to indicate the average wind power and wind speed at various locations in the South Central, East Central, and Southeast Regions. Included are all locations in these regions where wind speeds have been reliably measured over a long enough period to provide meaningful data. In these tables, wind power and wind speed are estimated at a height of 33 feet above ground level—the standard height for wind measurements. The 33-ft estimates are based on measurements taken at various ground levels. Since wind speed increases by about 1 mph for each 35 feet of elevation above ground, the average wind speed at the preferred level of wind machine installation (60 to 100 ft) is approximately 1 to 2 mph greater than that shown in these tables.

ESTIMATING A WIND MACHINE'S REDUCTION OF ELECTRIC BILLS

This Atlas makes it possible for you to estimate the amount of money you can save on electric bills by operating a wind machine. You need to know only three things:

1. *The wind speed class for the area where the wind machine will be installed.* Find your location on your state map to determine

the appropriate wind speed class. Use either the map that shows the annual average wind speed class or the map that applies to the season in which you are interested.
2. *The rating of the wind machine you are considering purchasing.* Wind machines are rated by the maximum amount of electricity (in kilowatts, or kW) that they can produce when the wind is blowing strongly. Wind machines rated at from 4 to 10 kW provide a substantial fraction of the electricity used by the average household. A 4-kW wind machine costs about $10,000 (installed); a 10-kW wind machine, about $25,000. Of course, prices may be higher or lower depending upon the manufacturer, the height of the tower supporting the machine, the difficulty of installation, and many other factors.
3. *The cost of electricity in your area.* To determine that cost, call your electric company or look at your bill, and divide the total bill by the number of kilowatt-hours used. The cost should be calculated in *cents* per kilowatt-hour (not dollars per kilowatt-hour).

Now, to calculate the amount that your wind machine will reduce your *monthly* electric bills, multiply as follows:

$$\begin{pmatrix} \text{Wind} \\ \text{Speed} \\ \text{Class} \end{pmatrix} \times \begin{pmatrix} \text{Wind Machine} \\ \text{Rating in} \\ \text{Kilowatts} \end{pmatrix} \times \begin{pmatrix} \text{Electricity Cost} \\ \text{in Cents per} \\ \text{Kilowatt-Hour} \end{pmatrix} \times \begin{pmatrix} \text{Units} \\ \text{Factor*} \\ \text{of 0.5} \end{pmatrix} = \begin{pmatrix} \text{Dollars} \\ \text{Saved} \\ \text{Per Month} \end{pmatrix}$$

Example: 3 × 4 × 7 × 0.5 = $42.00

A wind machine rated at 4 kW was used in this example. A 10-kW machine would save approximately $105.00 per month.

This calculation is only an approximation of the actual amount of money you can save. For example, remember that the wind speed class shown by this Atlas is only an estimate of the actual wind speed at your location. Wind speeds should be measured for at least three months before you decide on the machine best suited to your needs. Other factors that may affect the amount of money you can save are the following:

1. *The wind machine should be connected to available electric power lines.* The calculation of money saved is valid only when the wind machine is installed in such a way that it can feed power into the utility lines when you don't require the power. Federal law requires utilities to buy your wind-produced electricity at a cost that is only slightly lower than what you must

---

*The units factor is always 0.5.

pay to buy conventional electricity from the utility. If your wind machine is in a remote area, or if you don't take the trouble to hook it up to utility lines, the wasted electricity can cost you 50 percent or more of your savings. Of course, if you have a very small wind machine (rated at less than 1 kW), no electricity (or money) will be wasted. The same holds true if your house or business is so large that it uses as much power as your wind machine can generate.

2. *Raising the wind machine higher above the ground will increase savings.* The calculation of savings is based on a wind machine height of about 60 feet above ground level—the height recommended by many wind machine manufacturers. Since wind speed increases in accordance with height above ground, an increase in the height of your wind machine from 60 to 100 ft, for example, could increase savings by 30 percent.

    Wind speed increases most rapidly with height over forested or hilly terrain. It is important to install your wind machine so that its blades completely clear the level of the tallest trees, even if those trees are hundreds of feet away. Placing your machine atop the highest hill in the area (or nearly the highest) can increase savings substantially beyond those calculated because an exposed hilltop may increase the wind speed dramatically. The increase of wind speed with height is least dramatic over flat, treeless ground and near oceans and large lakes. Even in these areas, however, considerable savings can be achieved by increasing the height of your tower.

    Of course, a higher tower costs more. An increase in tower height from 60 to 100 ft usually costs several thousand dollars. Since this cost is readily recovered, however, by the increased savings resulting from the availability of higher winds, many manufacturers now recommend that their wind machines be installed at 80 to 100 feet above ground level.

3. *Purchasing an efficient wind machine will increase savings.* Before shopping for a wind machine, learn how the efficiency of wind machines is determined. You will find that some of them, although equal in size and rating to others, are more efficient in converting wind to electricity. Since wind machine technology is still developing, some brands of machines are not only inefficient, but poorly constructed. These brands break down repeatedly and never repay their cost through electricity savings.

    Shop for a wind machine in terms of its efficiency and durability. Several well-constructed brands are available that will convert wind to electricity in a highly efficient manner that can mean years of electricity savings.

2
Southeast Central Region

- Missouri
- Arkansas
- Louisiana

GENERAL INFORMATION

Some parts of the Southeast Central Region—for example, in western Missouri and over the Mississippi River Delta in Louisiana—have wind speeds that are marginally strong enough for economical production of energy by a wind machine. In fact, sites atop the ridges and peaks of the Ouachita and Ozark Mountains in Arkansas, which experience a yearly average of Class 4 winds, are quite favorable for energy production. Over the remainder of the three states, however, winds are too light for profitable wind machine operation (Class 1 and Class 2).

In the map of yearly average wind speeds in terms of wind speed classes shown in Fig. 1, the shaded portions indicate mountainous regions. The wind class values in these regions are valid only for ridge crests and mountain tops. Wind speeds in the intervening valleys in these shaded regions are not indicated, although it can be taken for granted that they are substantially lower than those on the mountain crests.

The seasons when winds are at their strongest is shown in Fig. 2. Spring is the windiest season over most of the South Central Region, but winter winds are strongest in some of the eastern parts of the three states, most especially in Louisiana.

8 SOUTH AND SOUTHEAST WIND ATLAS

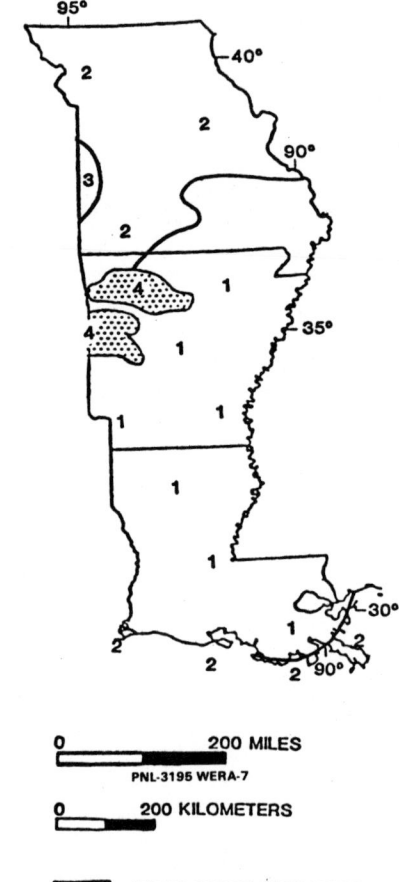

AVERAGE YEARLY WIND SPEED (MPH)	CORRESPONDING WIND SPEED CLASS
Below 9.8	1
9.8–11.5	2
11.6–12.5	3
12.6–13.4	4
13.5–14.3	5
14.4–15.7	6
Above 15.7	7

Fig. 1 Yearly average wind speeds in Southeast Central Region.

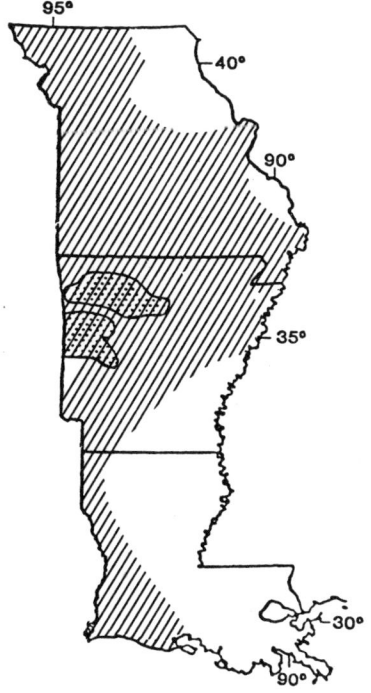

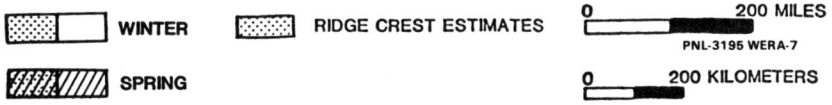

AVERAGE YEARLY WIND SPEED (MPH)	CORRESPONDING WIND SPEED CLASS
Below 9.8	1
9.8–11.5	2
11.6–12.5	3
12.6–13.4	4
13.5–14.3	5
14.4–15.7	6
Above 15.7	7

Fig. 2 Seasons of maximum wind speeds in Southeast Central Region.

MISSOURI

YEARLY AVERAGE WIND SPEEDS

Winds in Missouri are only marginally strong enough for the economical generation of energy. The map of yearly average wind speeds over the state in Fig. 3 indicates that the west central part of the state has the strongest winds—Class 3 (11.5 to 12.5 mph). The lowest wind speeds are in the southeast, where only Class 1 winds are found. The greater part of the state experiences Class 2 winds.

Missouri not only has lower wind speeds than the plains states to the west, but good wind machine sites are harder to find because of wooded and hilly terrain. The southern part of the state is particularly hilly, being an extension of the Ozark Mountains to the south. As a consequence, light winds prevail in the valleys and favorable winds over the high terrain and the hilltops. In the northern part of the state, the hills are somewhat lower and less numerous, resulting in Class 2 winds over more sites than are offered by the hillier Class 2 terrain to the south.

SEASONAL AVERAGE WIND SPEEDS

Missouri winds are strongest in the spring and weakest in the summer, as shown by the map of winter and summer wind speed classes in Fig. 4 and of autumn and spring wind speed classes in Fig. 5. Spring winds are as strong as Class 4 in the extreme north central and west central parts of the state, and no part experiences less than Class 2 winds. In contrast, in the following season—summer—winds do not exceed Class 1 in any part of the state. In autumn, winds rate Class 2 only in the north and west central parts but pick up considerably in winter, when about half of the state experiences Class 3 winds.

The monthly variations of wind speed are shown in Fig. 6 for four locations: Kansas City, St. Louis, Springfield, and Kirksville (the latter in north central Missouri). March is generally the windiest month and July or August the calmest at each of these cities. The difference between the windiest and least windy month is 4 to 5 mph at Kansas City and St. Louis and 6 to 7 mph at Springfield and Kirksville.

AVERAGE WIND SPEEDS BY DAY AND NIGHT

The average change of wind speed in Missouri by the hour of the day and night is typical of inland regions of low elevation. The weakest winds commonly blow near sunrise, followed by a rapid increase in speed until noon, a peak in the afternoon (early afternoon in winter and late afternoon in summer), a rapid decrease until an hour or two after sunset, and quite light winds during the nighttime hours. The change in wind speed by hour of the day is shown for Kansas City,

St. Louis, Kirksville, and Springfield in Fig. 7. Average winds increase from 8 or 9 mph at sunrise to 12 mph at midafternoon in Kansas City, St. Louis, and Springfield. At Kirksville, however, the day-night difference is only 2 mph—from a minimum of 11.5 mph to a maximum of 13.5 mph.

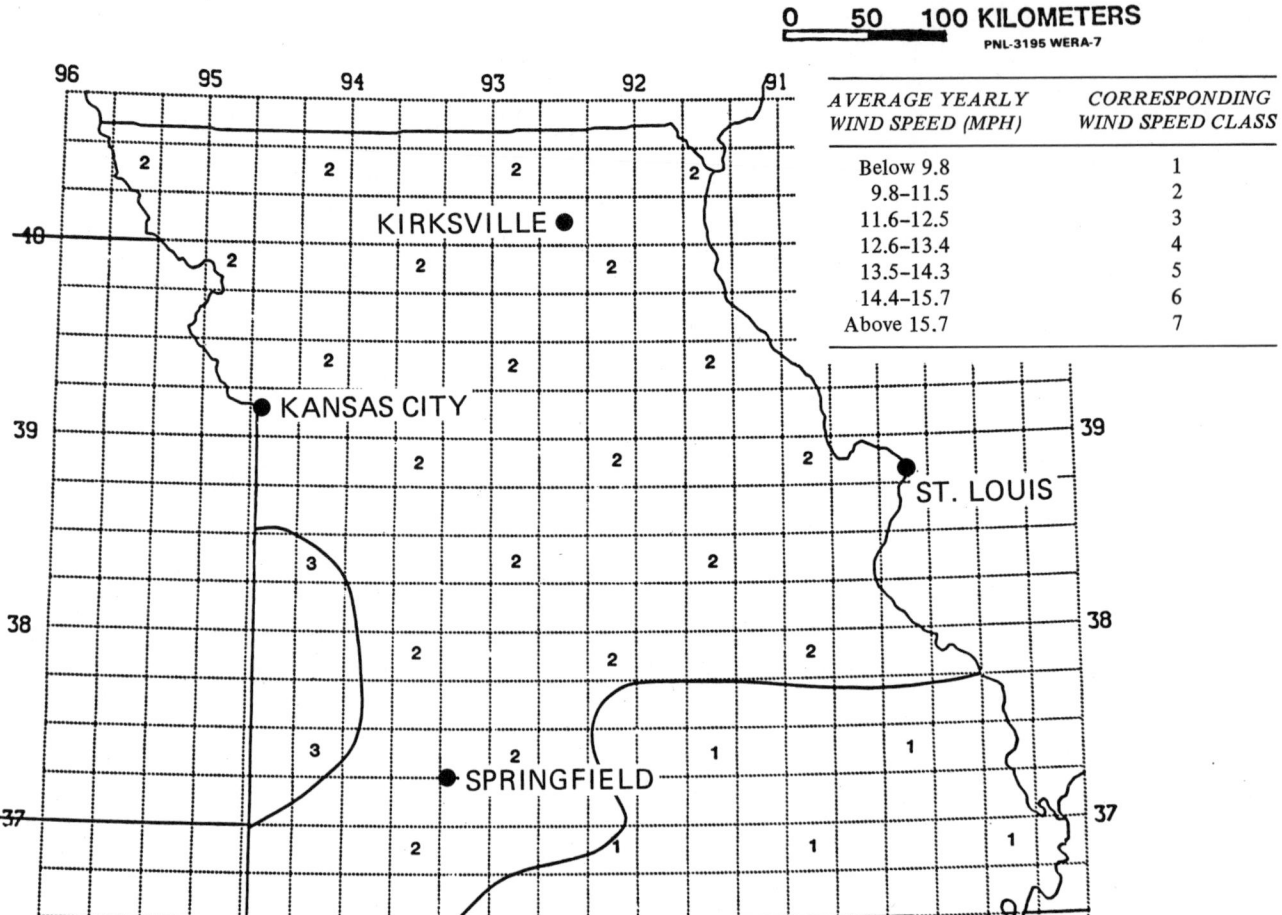

Fig. 3 Yearly average wind speeds in Missouri.

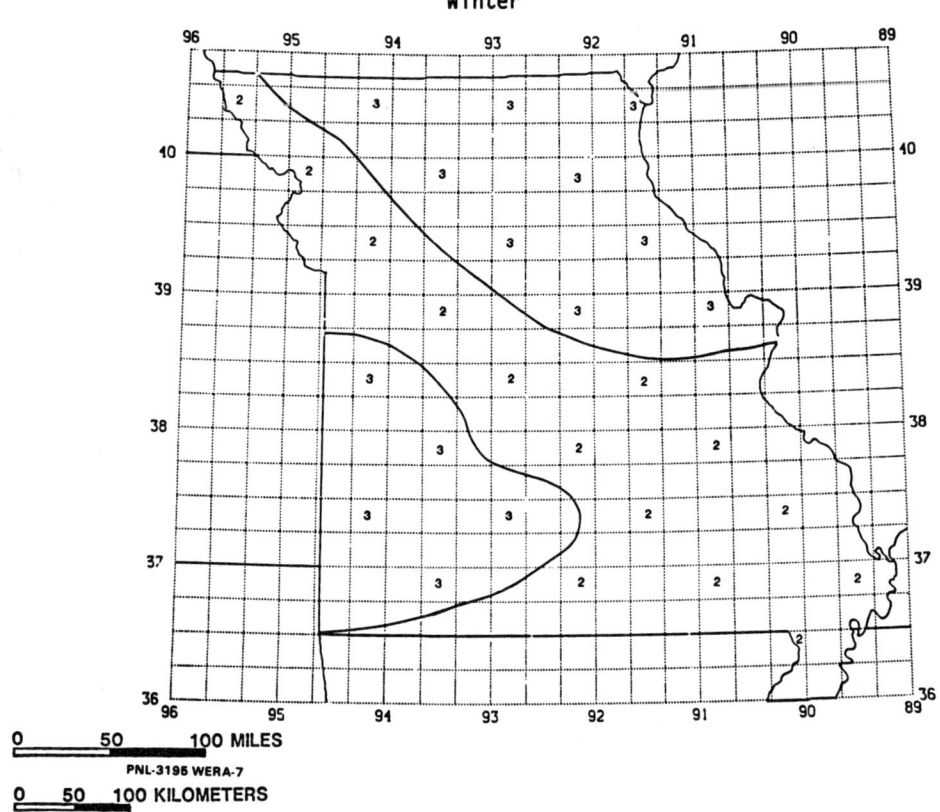

Fig. 4 Seasonal average wind speeds in Missouri.

14 SOUTH AND SOUTHEAST WIND ATLAS

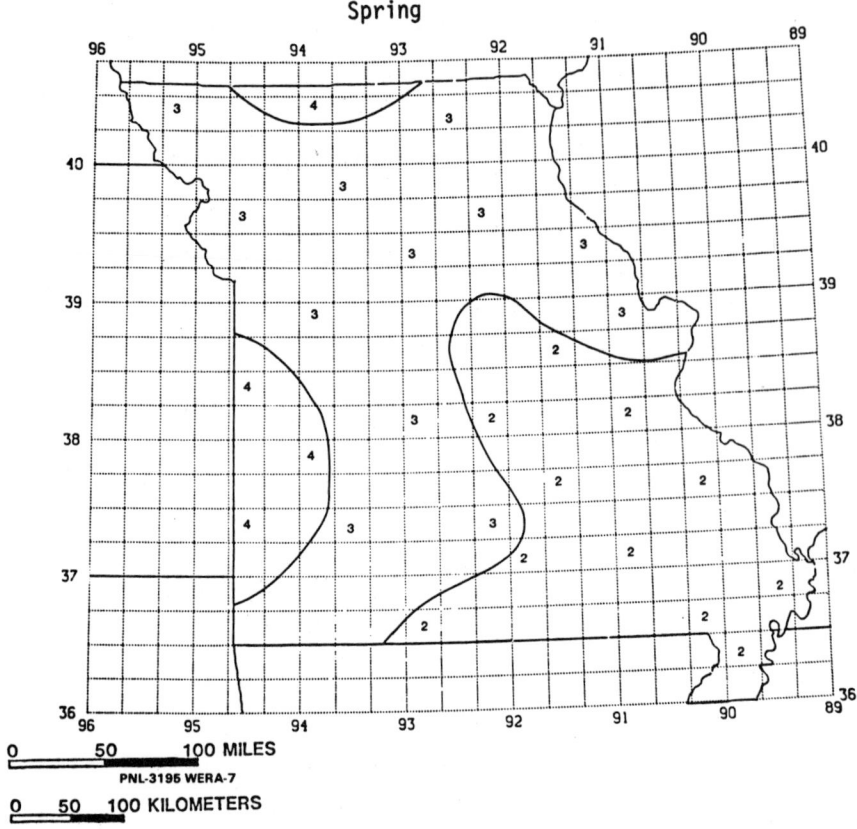

AVERAGE YEARLY WIND SPEED (MPH)	CORRESPONDING WIND SPEED CLASS
Below 9.8	1
9.8–11.5	2
11.6–12.5	3
12.6–13.4	4
13.5–14.3	5
14.4–15.7	6
Above 15.7	7

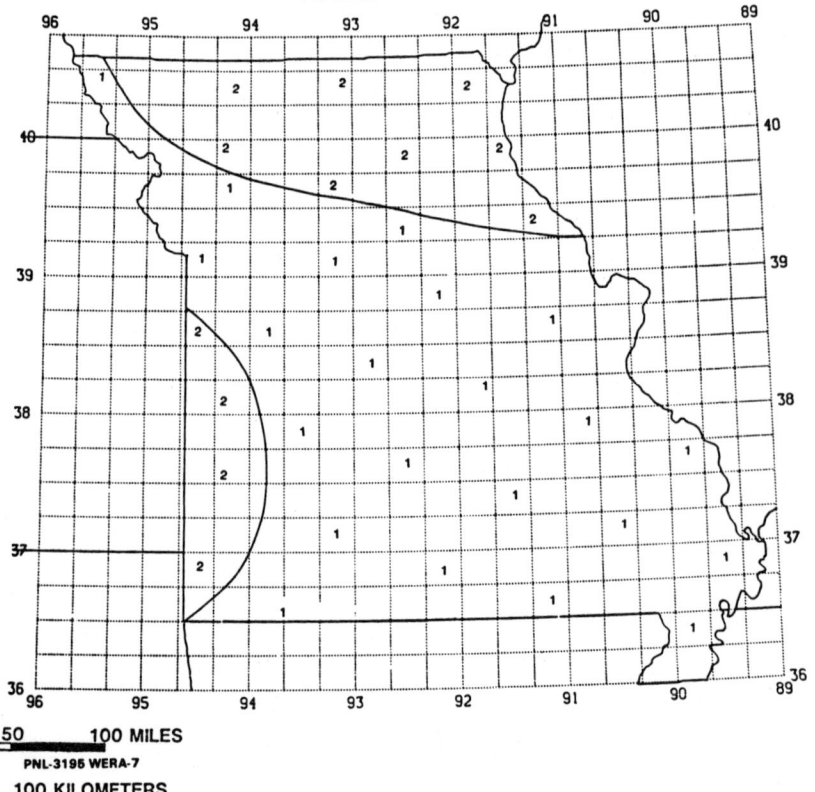

Fig. 5 Seasonal average wind speeds in Missouri.

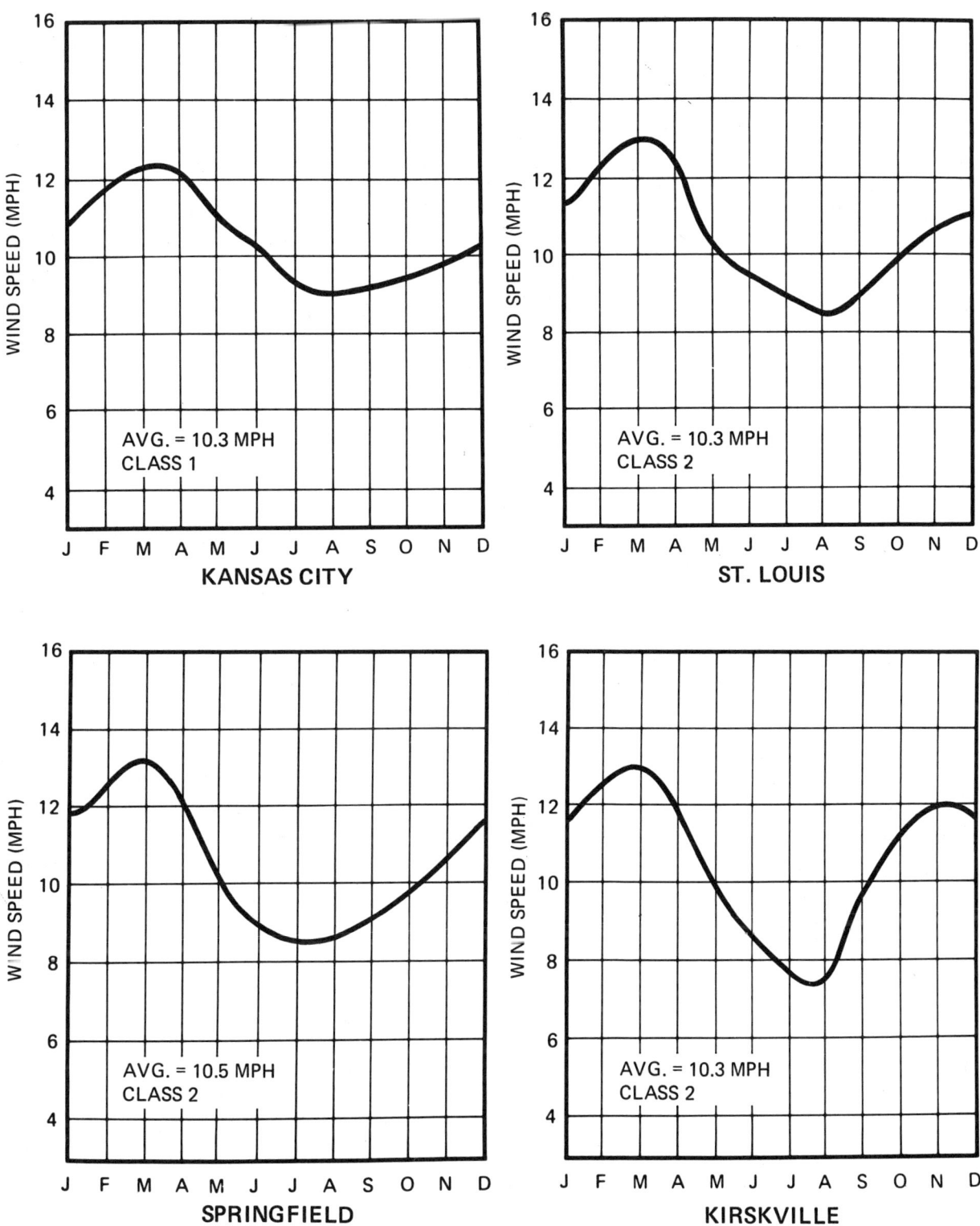

Fig. 6 Monthly average wind speeds in Missouri.

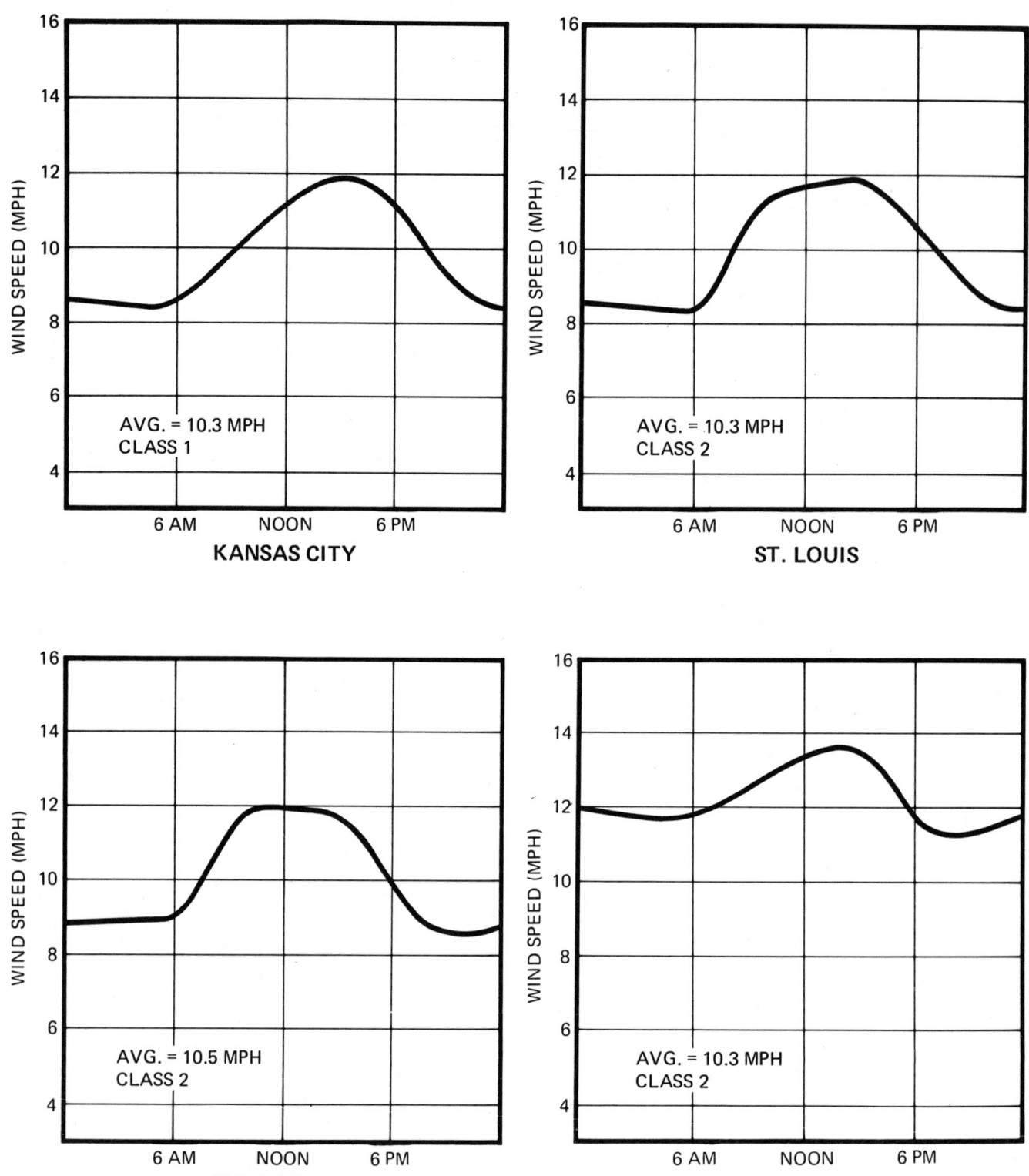

Fig. 7 Hourly average wind speeds in Missouri.

ARKANSAS

YEARLY AVERAGE WIND SPEEDS

In most parts of Arkansas, average wind speeds are lower than the minimum necessary to operate a wind machine profitably. Arkansas is too far south to benefit from the storm winds that buffet the northern states and too far east to benefit from the gusty winds of the great open plains to the west. As indicated in Fig. 8, which shows the yearly average wind speeds across the state, the only exceptions are the crests and summits of the Boston and Ouachita Mountains in the northwestern part of the state. The exposed mountain tops and ridges experience Class 4 (12.5 to 13.4 mph) winds, but the valleys and lower slopes are blocked from these stronger air currents and experience no more than the Class 1 winds that prevail in the rest of the state.

SEASONAL AVERAGE WIND SPEEDS

The variability of wind speeds in Arkansas between winter and summer is shown in Fig. 9; between spring and autumn, in Fig. 10. Winter and spring are clearly the windiest seasons. Winds on the crests of the Boston and Ouachita Mountains reach Class 5 in winter and Class 4 in spring. At lower elevations, a touch of the blustery spring winds more typical of regions farther north is suggested by the Class 3 winds in the extreme northwestern part of the state. Winds are Class 2 in both winter and spring away from the mountains in the northeastern half of the state. In southern and western Arkansas, as well as in the Arkansas Valley, winds fail to average more than Class 1 during any season.

Average monthly winds over the course of the four seasons at Little Rock, Blytheville, Texarkana, and Ft. Smith are shown in Fig. 11. Wind speeds peak at 9 to 11 mph during March or April at each location and then fall to 5 to 7 mph in July and August. At none of these cities are winds strong enough to average more than Class 1 for the year as a whole.

AVERAGE WIND SPEEDS BY DAY AND NIGHT

Arkansas winds average 3 to 4 mph stronger during the early afternoon than at night, as shown by Fig. 12, which provides the hourly average wind speed at Little Rock, Blytheville, Texarkana, and Ft. Smith. At each location, winds rise abruptly during the forenoon, after having reached a minimum at sunrise. Peak wind speeds occur around 2 P.M.—a little earlier during winter and a bit later during summer—and decrease quickly to their nighttime minimum at about 9 P.M.

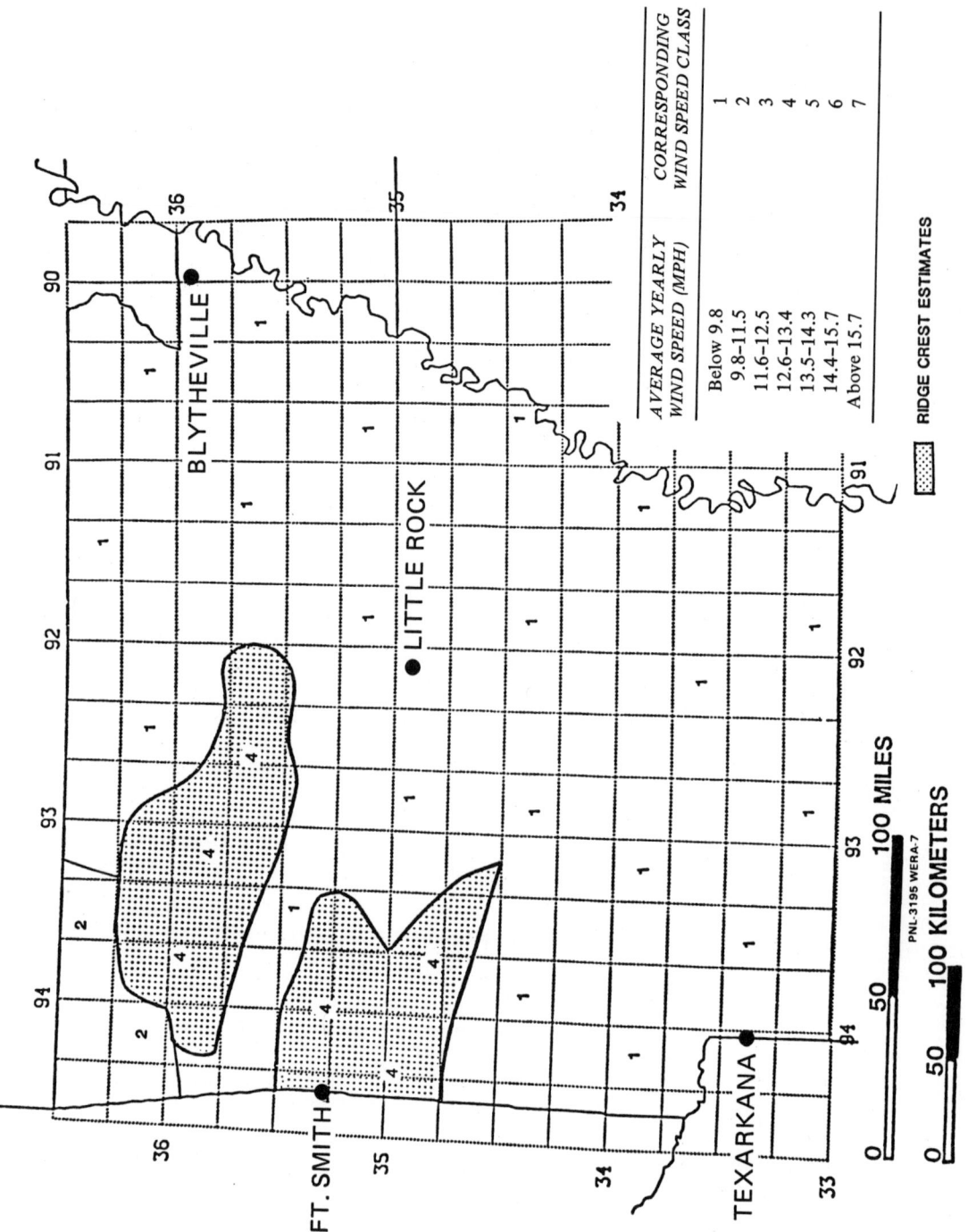

Fig. 8 Yearly average wind speeds in Arkansas.

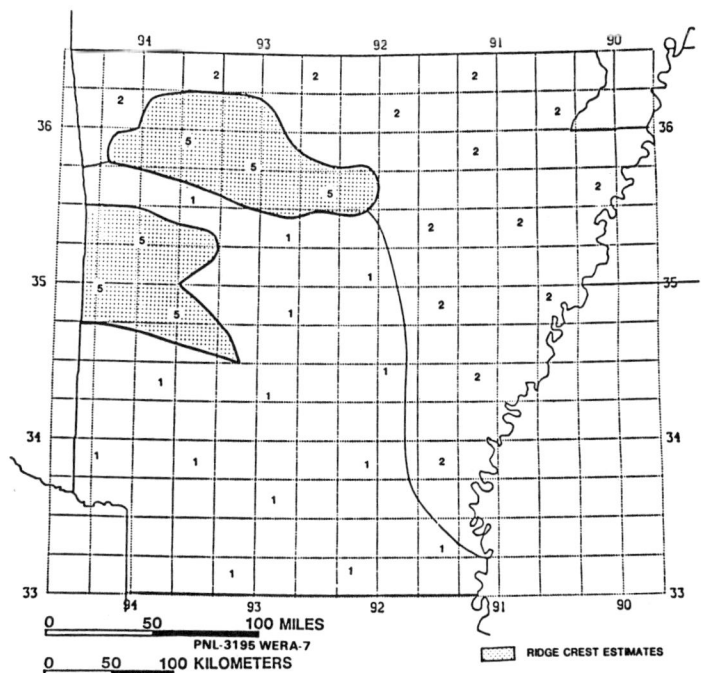

AVERAGE YEARLY WIND SPEED (MPH)	CORRESPONDING WIND SPEED CLASS
Below 9.8	1
9.8–11.5	2
11.6–12.5	3
12.6–13.4	4
13.5–14.3	5
14.4–15.7	6
Above 15.7	7

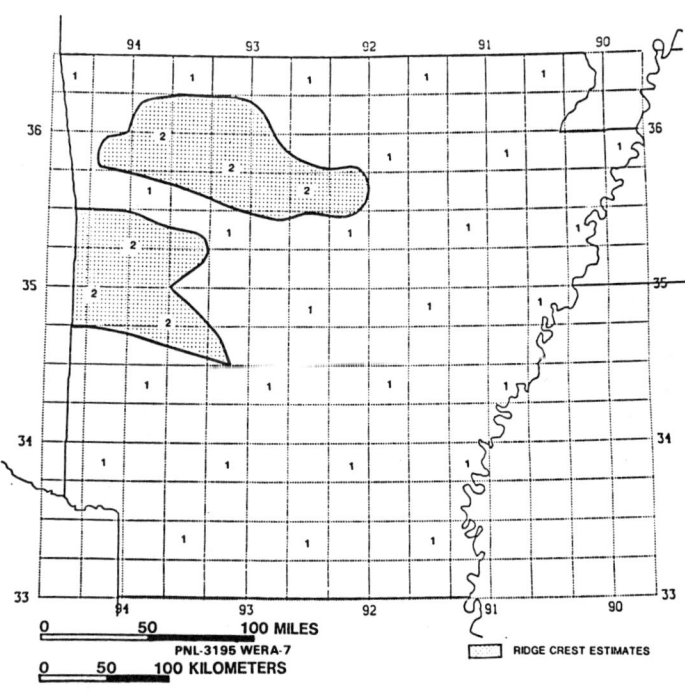

Fig. 9 Seasonal average wind speeds in Arkansas.

20 SOUTH AND SOUTHEAST WIND ATLAS

AVERAGE YEARLY WIND SPEED (MPH)	CORRESPONDING WIND SPEED CLASS
Below 9.8	1
9.8–11.5	2
11.6–12.5	3
12.6–13.4	4
13.5–14.3	5
14.4–15.7	6
Above 15.7	7

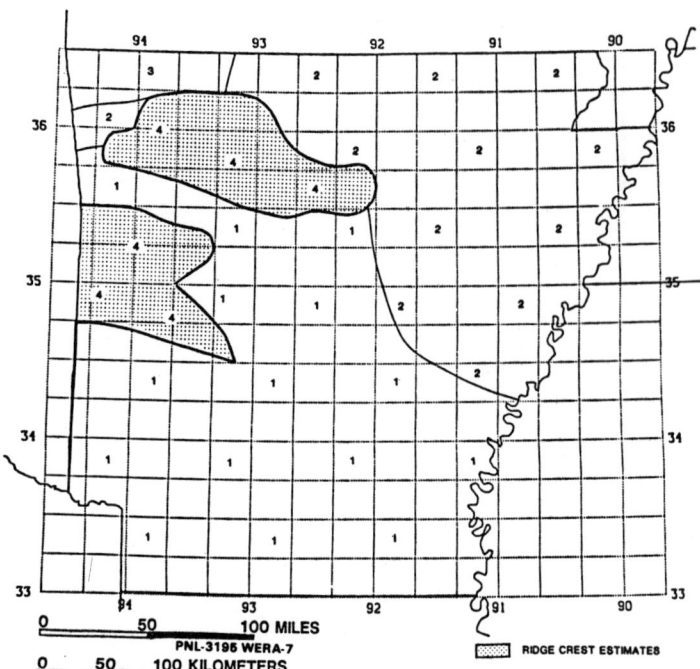

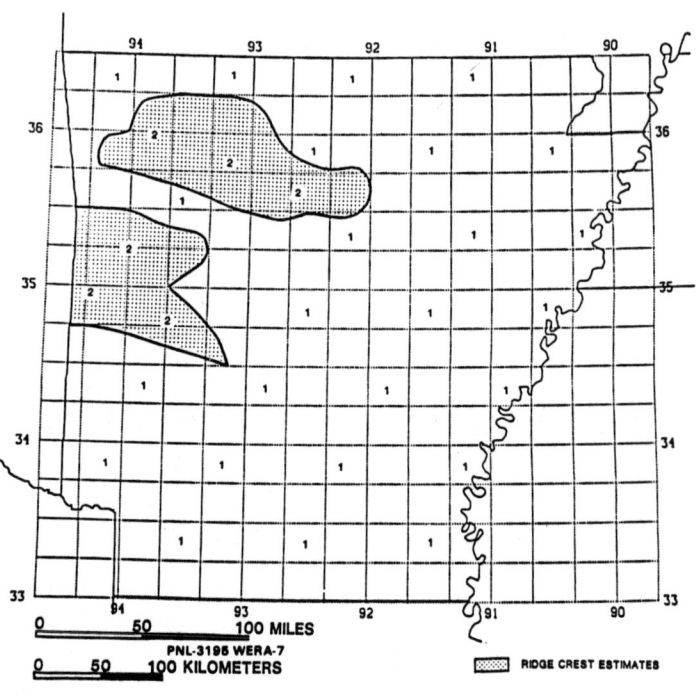

Fig. 10 Seasonal average wind speeds in Arkansas.

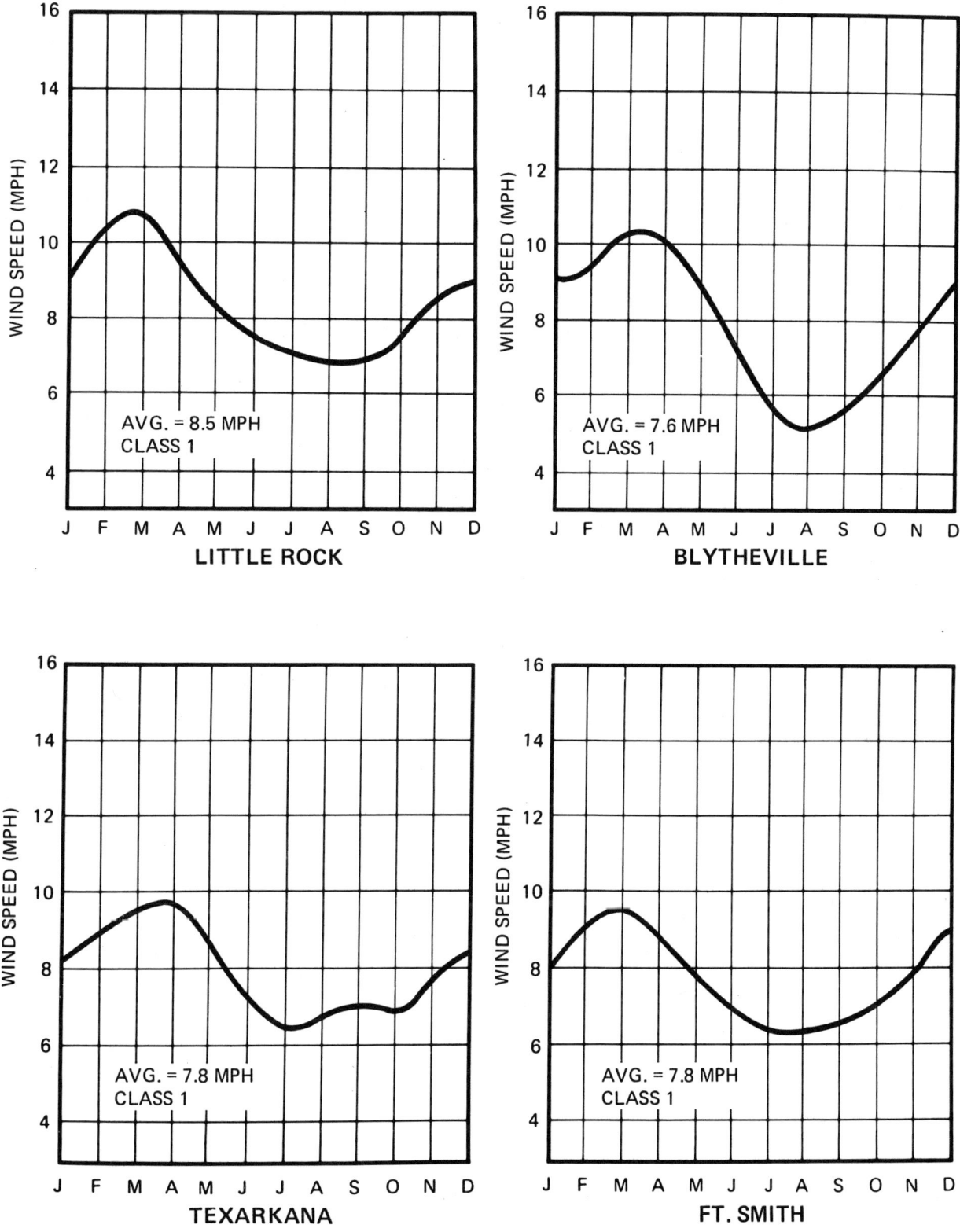

Fig. 11 Monthly average wind speeds in Arkansas.

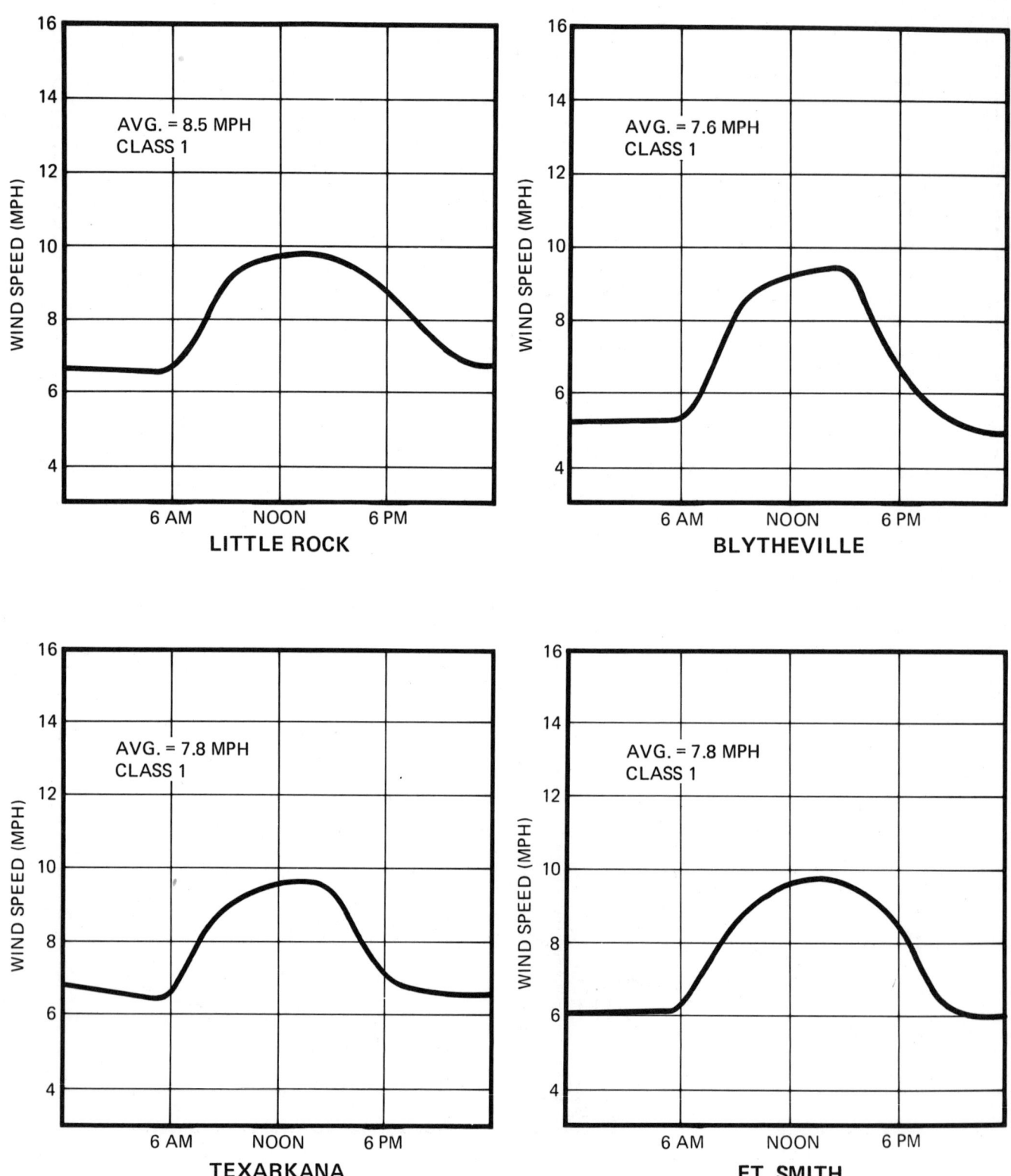

Fig. 12 Hourly average wind speeds in Arkansas.

LOUISIANA

YEARLY AVERAGE WIND SPEEDS

Wind speeds are too low for the siting of wind machines in almost the entire state (97 percent) of Louisiana, as suggested by Fig. 13. The forests that cover much of this Deep South state further reduce the already weak winds that do arise. Only the coastline directly exposed to the Gulf of Mexico and the outer Mississippi Delta experience winds as high as Class 2.

SEASONAL AVERAGE WIND SPEEDS

Average wind speeds are shown for winter and summer in Fig. 14; for spring and autumn, in Fig. 15. More than 30 miles from the Gulf Coast, winds are stronger in winter than in summer but average no more than Class 1 in any season. Class 2 winds—marginal for practical wind machine operation—extend as far north as Lake Pontchartrain during winter and as far as New Orleans during spring. Over the extreme lower end of the Mississippi Delta, however, winter winds are as high as Class 4.

In autumn, winds are as high as Class 2 only along the gulf coastline and over the lower Delta; Class 1 winds are the rule elsewhere. In summer, Class 1 winds cover the entire state. Average wind speeds for each month are shown for New Orleans, Shreveport, Lake Charles, and Burrwood in Fig. 16. Shreveport is typical of inland locations, Lake Charles of the waning influence of winds from the Gulf Coast, New Orleans of upper delta locations, and Burrwood of the relatively windy lower delta.

Wind speeds are strongest during March except at Burrwood, where they are strongest during midwinter. Midsummer winds average only 6 to 7 mph during the sultry days of July and August at the first three locations but nearly 8 mph at Burrwood.

AVERAGE WIND SPEEDS BY DAY AND NIGHT

Wind speeds vary from day to night by approximately 4 to 5 mph over most of Louisiana, as shown in Fig. 17 for the four locations: Lake Charles, New Orleans, Shreveport, and Burrwood. At inland locations, the wind speed minimum normally occurs at dawn; the maximum, in early afternoon. The difference between night and day is slightly greater during spring and early summer than in late autumn and winter.

At Burrwood—which is so nearly surrounded by the Gulf of Mexico that for all practical purposes it may be considered located in the Gulf itself—there is very little difference between daytime and nighttime wind speeds. The same is also true, but to a lesser extent, of all locations on the immediate Gulf Coast.

24 SOUTH AND SOUTHEAST WIND ATLAS

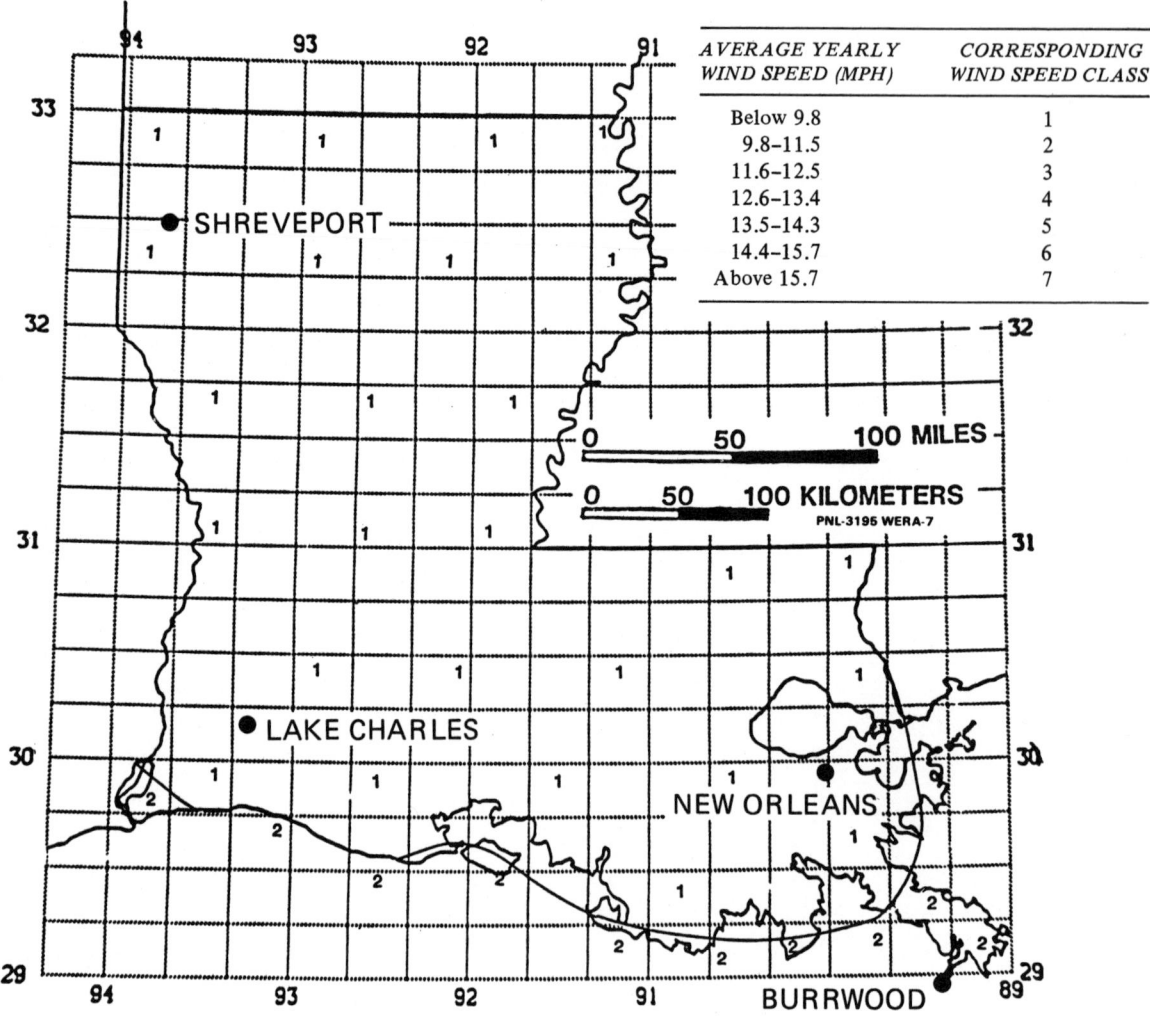

Fig. 13 Yearly average wind speeds in Louisiana.

AVERAGE YEARLY WIND SPEED (MPH)	CORRESPONDING WIND SPEED CLASS
Below 9.8	1
9.8–11.5	2
11.6–12.5	3
12.6–13.4	4
13.5–14.3	5
14.4–15.7	6
Above 15.7	7

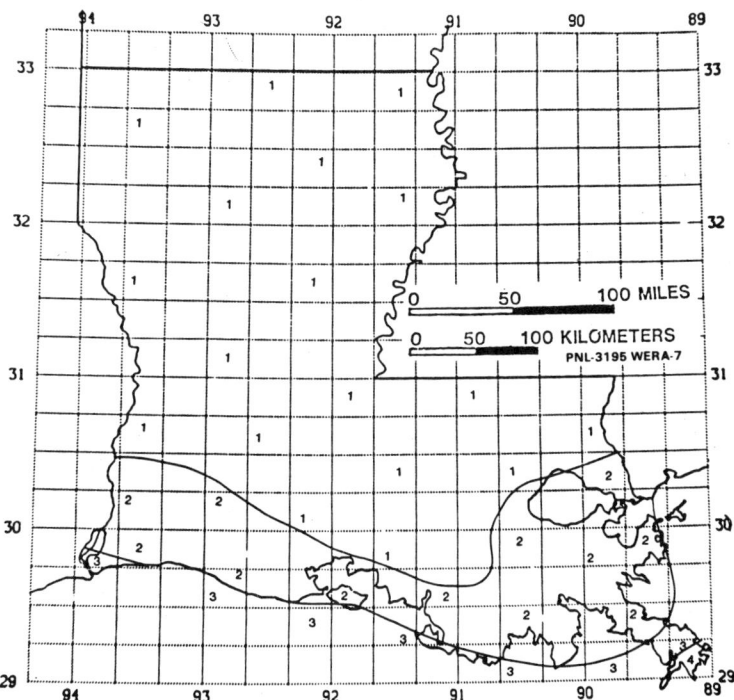

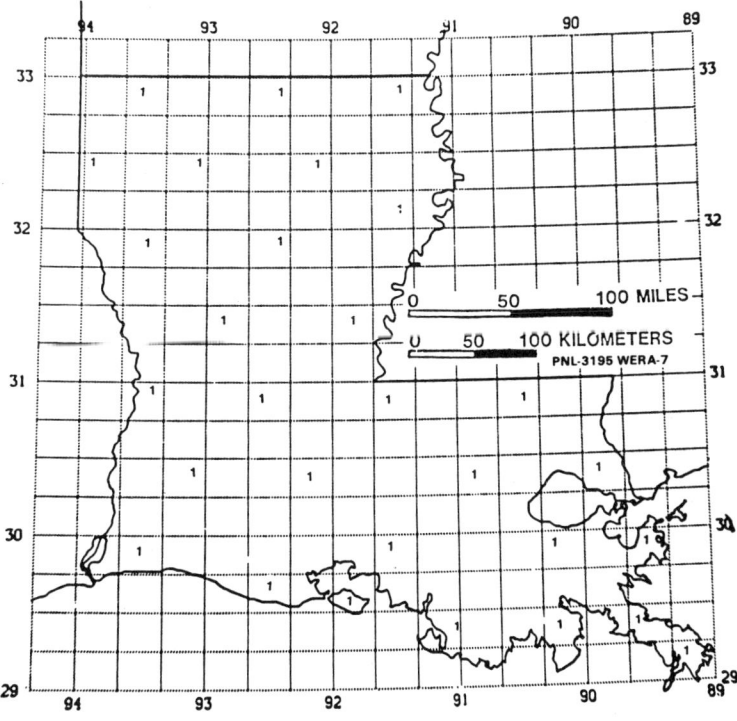

Fig. 14 Seasonal average wind speeds in Louisiana.

26 SOUTH AND SOUTHEAST WIND ATLAS

AVERAGE YEARLY WIND SPEED (MPH)	CORRESPONDING WIND SPEED CLASS
Below 9.8	1
9.8–11.5	2
11.6–12.5	3
12.6–13.4	4
13.5–14.3	5
14.4–15.7	6
Above 15.7	7

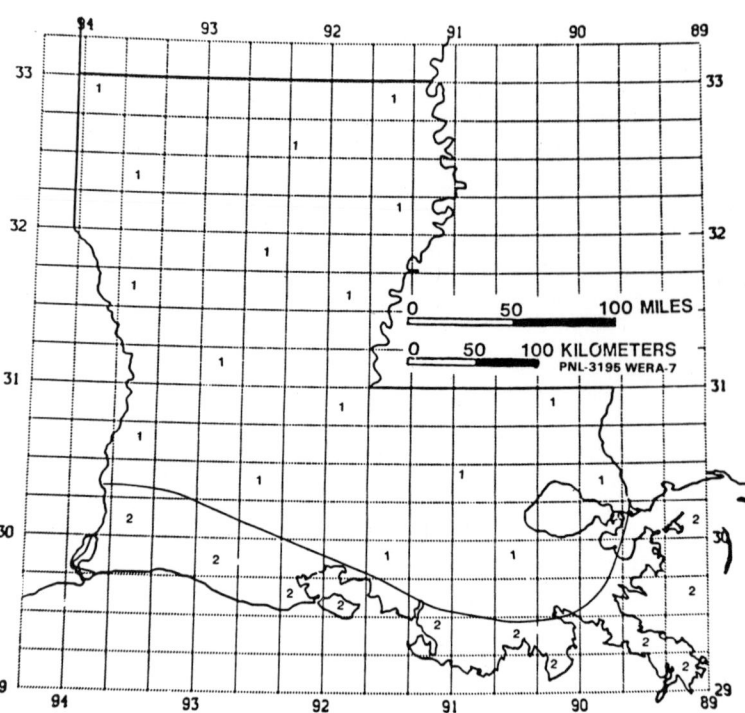

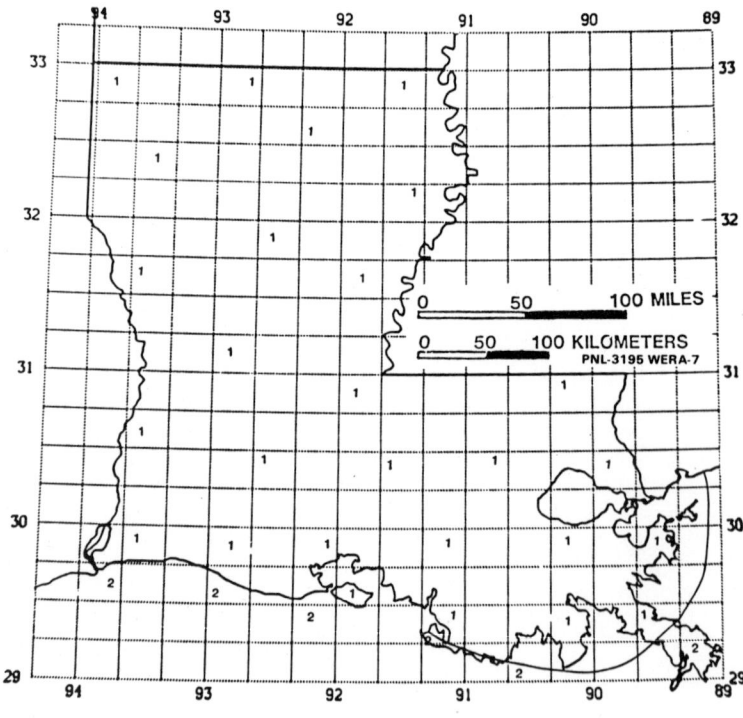

Fig. 15 Seasonal average wind speeds in Louisiana.

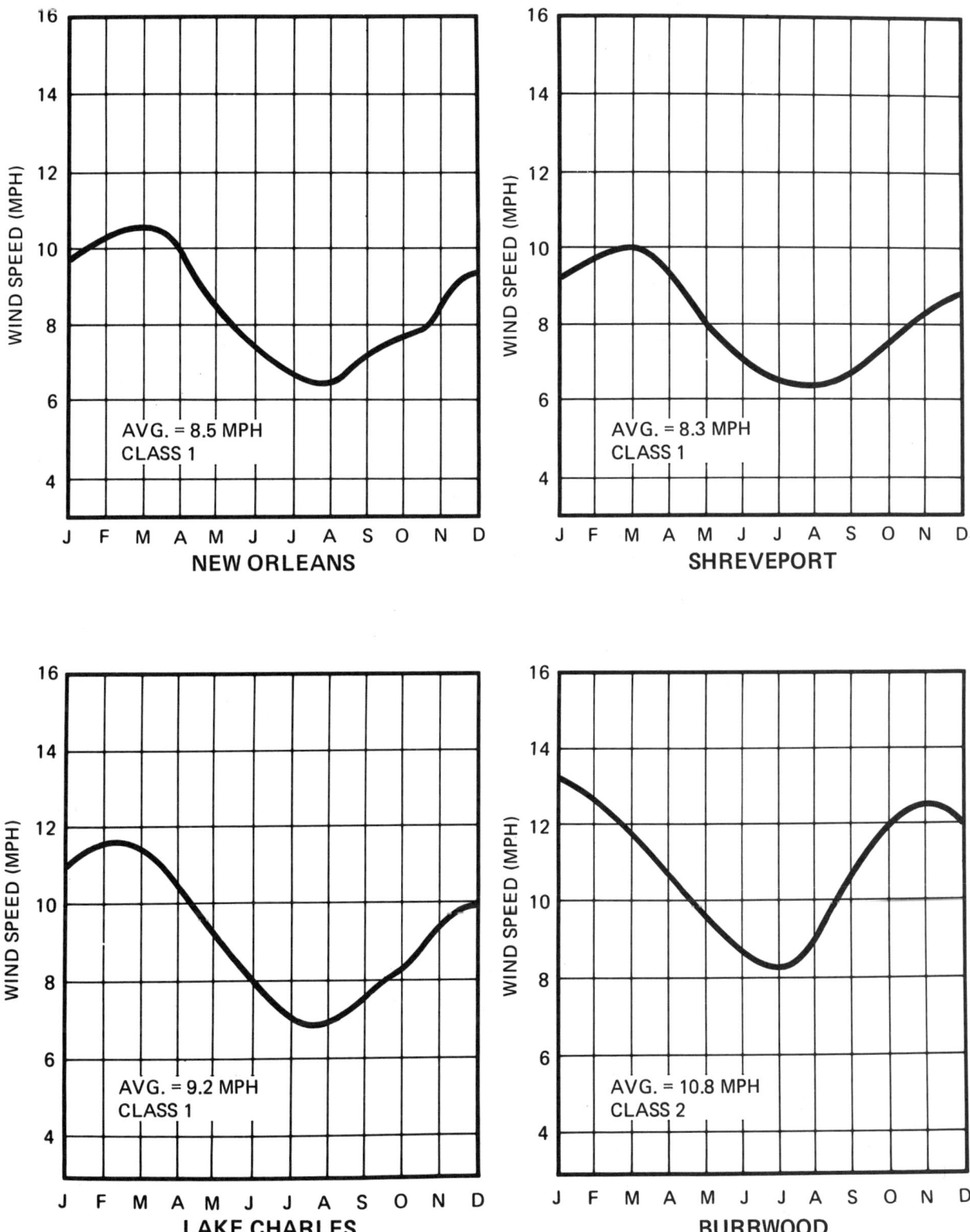

Fig. 16 Monthly average wind speeds in Louisiana.

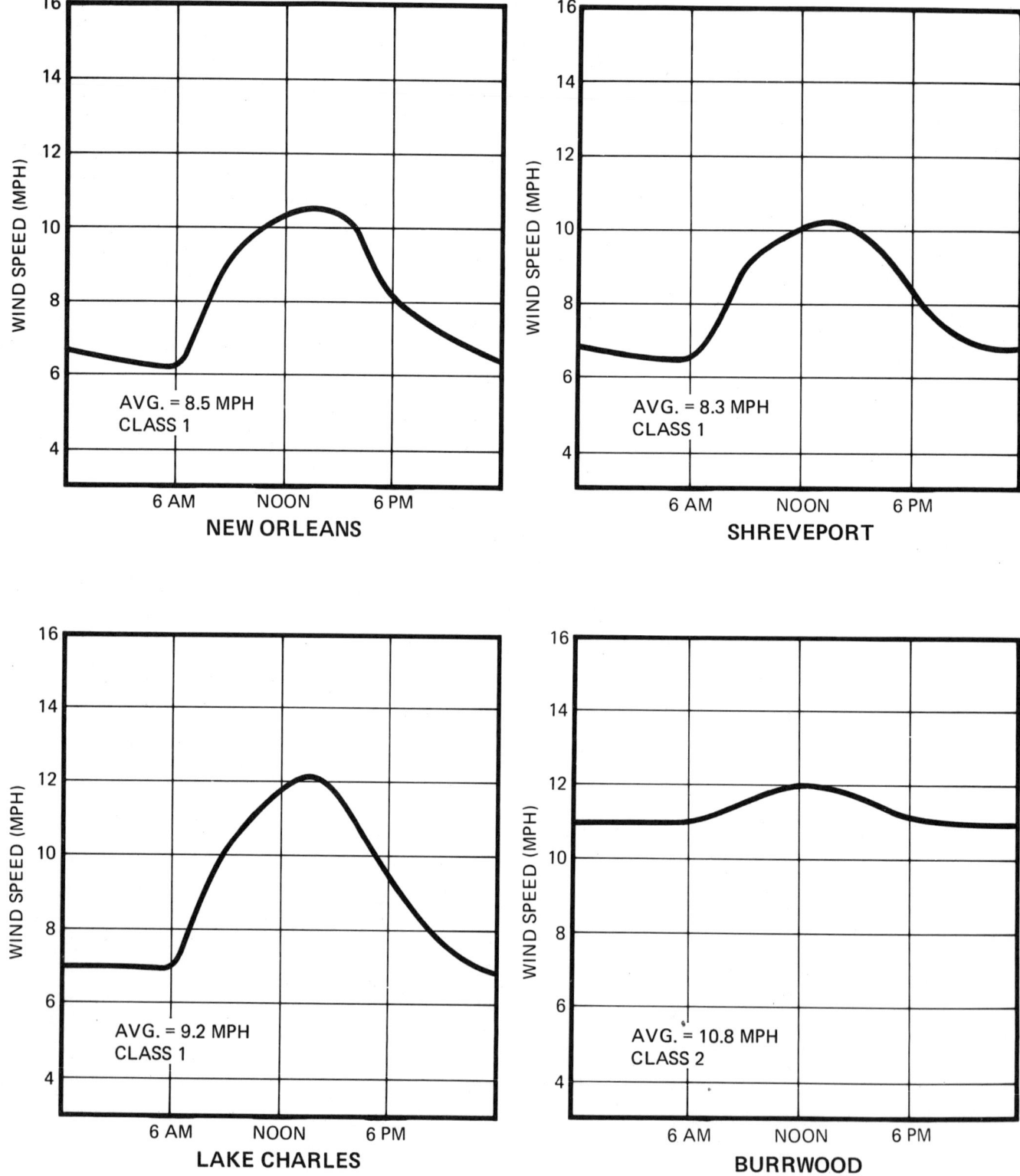

Fig. 17 Hourly average wind speeds in Louisiana.

WIND SPEED AND WIND POWER AT VARIOUS LOCATIONS IN THE SOUTHEAST CENTRAL REGION

The table that follows shows the yearly average wind speed and the yearly average wind power at each location in the Southeast Central Region where winds are measured frequently and reliably. Not enough measurements have been made at other locations to provide the basis for computing reliable yearly averages. (For a definition of wind power and its relationship to average wind speed, refer to page 3.)

SOUTH AND SOUTHEAST WIND ATLAS

TOWN, CITY, OR PLACE	FACILITY	YEARLY AVERAGE WIND SPEED (MPH AT 33 FT ABOVE GROUND)	YEARLY AVERAGE WIND POWER (WATTS PER SQ. METER)
MISSOURI			
Advance	Advance Civil Aeronautics Adm.	8.3	74
Butler	Butler Civil Aeronautics Adm.	11.0	159
Chillicothe	Chillicothe Civil Aeronautics Adm.	10.8	127
Columbia	Columbia Municipal Airport	9.9	93
Farmington	Farmington Civil Aeronautics Adm.	8.3	69
Ft. Leonard Wood	Ft. Leonard Wood Army Air Field	8.3	86
Grandview	Richards-Gebaur Air Force Base	9.2	92
Joplin	Joplin Airport	11.6	159
Kansas City	Kansas City Municipal Airport	10.3	99
Kirksville	Cannon Memorial Airport	10.3	104
Malden	Malden Civil Aeronautics Adm.	9.2	95
Marshall	Marshall Civil Aeronautics Adm.	9.2	88
New Florence	New Florence Civil Aeronautics Adm.	11.6	129
St. Joseph	St. Joseph Airport	9.9	120
St. Louis	Lambert Field	10.3	114
Springfield	Springfield Municipal Airport	10.5	109
Tarkio	Tarkio Civil Aeronautics Adm.	7.8	99
Vichy	Vichy Airport	9.4	77
ARKANSAS			
Blytheville	Blytheville Air Force Base	6.9	78
El Dorado	Goodwin Airport	7.4	48
Fayetteville	Fayetteville Airport	8.5	78
Flippin	Flippin Civil Aeronautic Adm.	6.5	42
Ft. Smith	Ft. Smith Municipal Airport	7.4	54
Harrison	Harrison Airport	9.0	82
Jacksonville	Little Rock Air Force Base	5.4	46
Little Rock	Adams Field	7.8	66
Pine Bluff	Grider Field	7.6	59
Texarkana	Webb Field	7.6	58
Walnut Ridge	Municipal Airport	7.2	64
LOUISIANA			
Alexandria	Esler Field Airport	6.7	52
Baton Rouge	Ryan Field Airport	8.3	67
Boothville	Boothville Weather Bureau Office	9.4	96

TOWN, CITY, OR PLACE	FACILITY	YEARLY AVERAGE WIND SPEED (MPH AT 33 FT ABOVE GROUND)	YEARLY AVERAGE WIND POWER (WATTS PER SQ. METER)
	LOUISIANA (continued)		
Burrwood	Burrwood Special Purpose Office	10.8	139
Ft. Polk	Ft. Polk Army Air Field	6.7	45
Lafayette	Lafayette Municipal Airport	7.6	59
Lake Charles	Lake Charles Airport	9.2	87
Monroe	Monroe Airport	7.6	65
New Iberia	New Iberia Airport	4.3	17
New Orleans	Moisant International Airport	8.5	72
New Orleans	New Orleans Naval Air Station	6.0	45
Shreveport	Shreveport Municipal Airport	8.3	62
Shreveport	Barksdale Air Force Base	6.5	52

3
East Central Region

- Kentucky
- Tennessee
- West Virginia
- Maryland–Delaware
- Virginia
- North Carolina

GENERAL INFORMATION

Although the East Central Region contains a number of areas with wind speeds high enough to make the operation of wind machines rewarding, wind speeds are marginal or too low over most of the region for that to be the case. A map of yearly average wind speeds for the seven states is shown in Fig. 18. The only two areas that offer wind speeds greater than Class 1 (more than 9.8 mph) are those adjacent to the Appalachian Mountains (shaded in Fig. 18) or the Atlantic Coast, especially to the north and west of the Appalachians and for some miles inland from the coast, including the furthest reaches of Chesapeake Bay. Class 3 and stronger winds (averaged over the four seasons) are confined to the mountain crests, where they may be as high as Class 6, and the immediate coast, where they may be as high as Class 4.

The seasons normally having the strongest winds in the East Central Region are shown in Fig. 19. Winter is the windiest season over all of the Appalachian Mountains and most of the region to the west as well as the entire area around Chesapeake Bay. Spring is the season of strongest winds to the east of the Appalachians (with the exception, of course, of Chesapeake Bay) and in the extreme western portions of Kentucky and Tennessee. The least windy season over the entire region is summer.

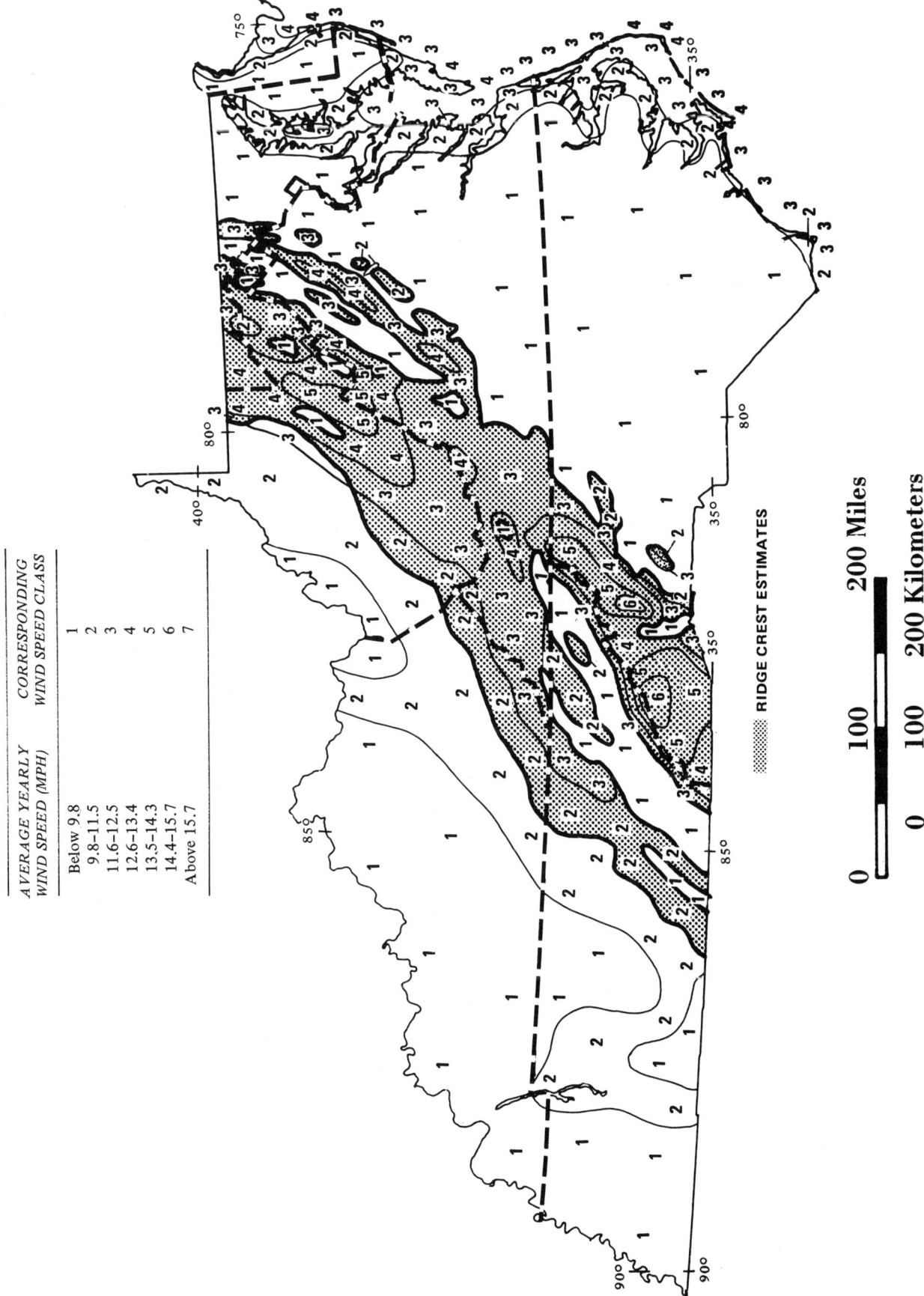

Fig. 18 Yearly average wind speeds in East Central Region.

34 SOUTH AND SOUTHEAST WIND ATLAS

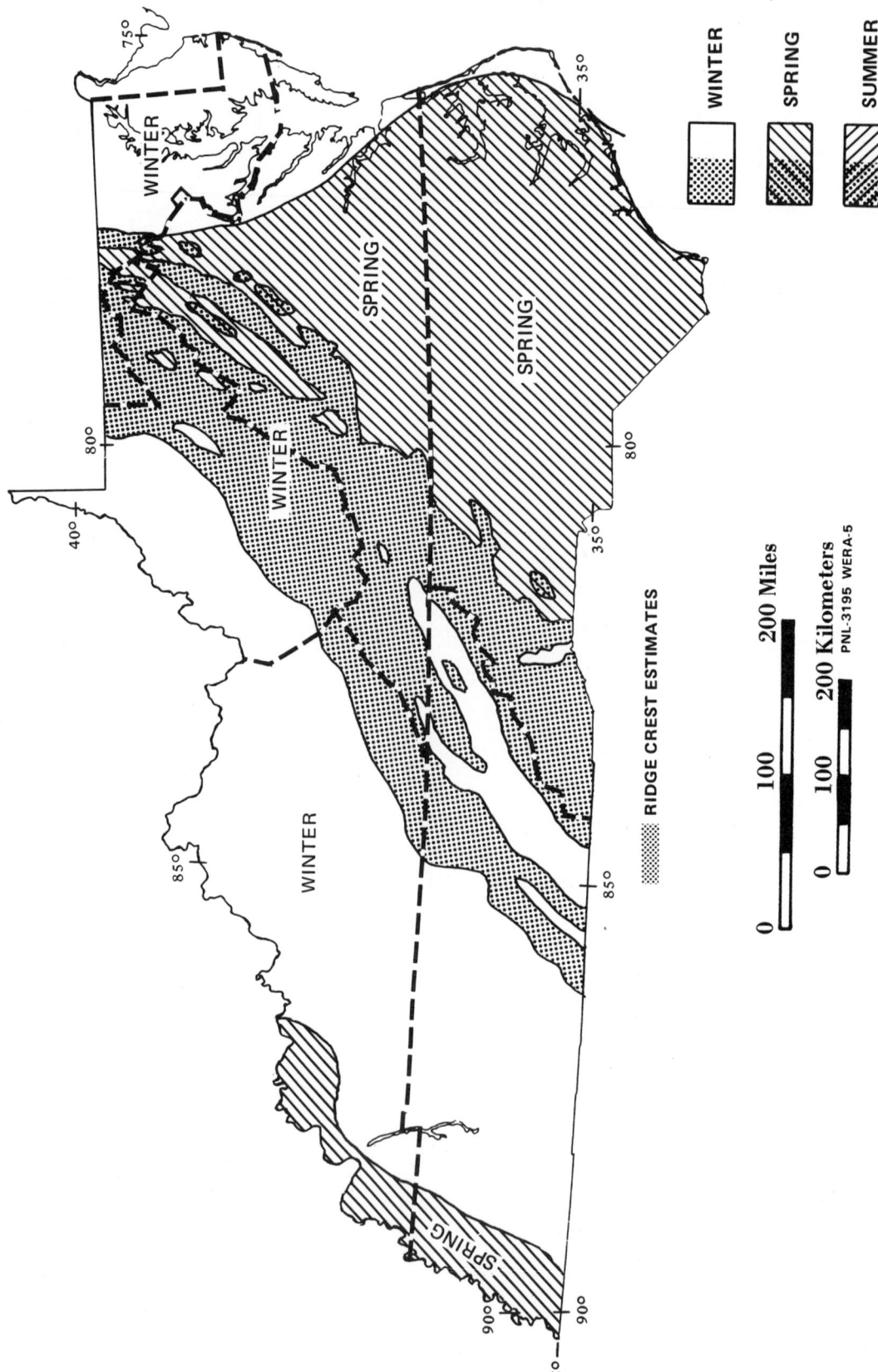

Fig. 19 Seasons of maximum wind speeds in East Central Region.

KENTUCKY

YEARLY AVERAGE WIND SPEEDS

The crests and summits of the Appalachian Mountains and their foothills in southeastern Kentucky are practically the only parts of the state where winds are stronger than Class 1 (more than 9.8 mph), as shown by the map of yearly average wind speeds in Fig. 20. The higher crests of the mountains near the Virginia border are the only ones that experience Class 3 winds. The lower ridges and hilltops, including those in the Pine Mountains, average Class 2 winds. The valleys and the lower slopes of the Appalachians (shaded area in Fig. 20), experience only Class 1 winds, as does the remainder of the state, except for a small region of Class 2 winds west of Kentucky Lake in the southwestern part of the state.

The extensive woods over much of the state reduce wind speeds below treetop height even in large cleared areas. Where woods are sparse—for example, over some of the hilltops in central and western Kentucky within the area marked Class 1 in Fig. 20—some Class 2 winds may occur.

SEASONAL AVERAGE WIND SPEEDS

Average wind speeds during winter and summer are shown in Fig. 21, and those during spring and autumn in Fig. 22. Winter and spring are by far the windiest seasons. Away from the mountains, Class 2 winds blow during both seasons. On top of the mountains, winter wind speeds—which reach a very respectable Class 6 on the highest ridges near the Virginia border—are about two classes higher than spring wind speeds.

Summer is a time of still air over both mountain and plain; both experience only Class 1 winds. Autumnal winds are scarcely any stronger; only the highest ridges manage to attain Class 2 status.

Monthly average wind speeds at Louisville, Lexington, Paducah, and Ft. Campbell (in southwestern Kentucky) are shown in Fig. 23. At all four locations, the strongest winds come in March and the weakest in July or August. The difference between the windiest and least windy month is 4 to 5 mph.

AVERAGE WIND SPEEDS BY DAY AND NIGHT

In Kentucky, winds are stronger during the day than they are at night, as is true of most parts of the United States. The lightest winds come, as a rule, between midnight and dawn, whereas the windiest time of day is early afternoon. The hourly variation of wind speeds at four Kentucky locations—Louisville, Lexington, Paducah, and Ft. Campbell—is shown in Fig. 24. At Louisville, Lexington, and Paducah, sunrise wind speeds average between 6 and 8 mph and increase to

10 to 11 mph at the afternoon peak. At Ft. Campbell, winds average only 4 mph at night and increase more than 100 percent to 8.5 mph in early afternoon.

Winds atop the higher ridges of the Appalachian Mountains may experience less variation between day and night. Measurements are lacking atop Kentucky ridges to confirm such a tendency, but it has been verified in other mountainous areas.

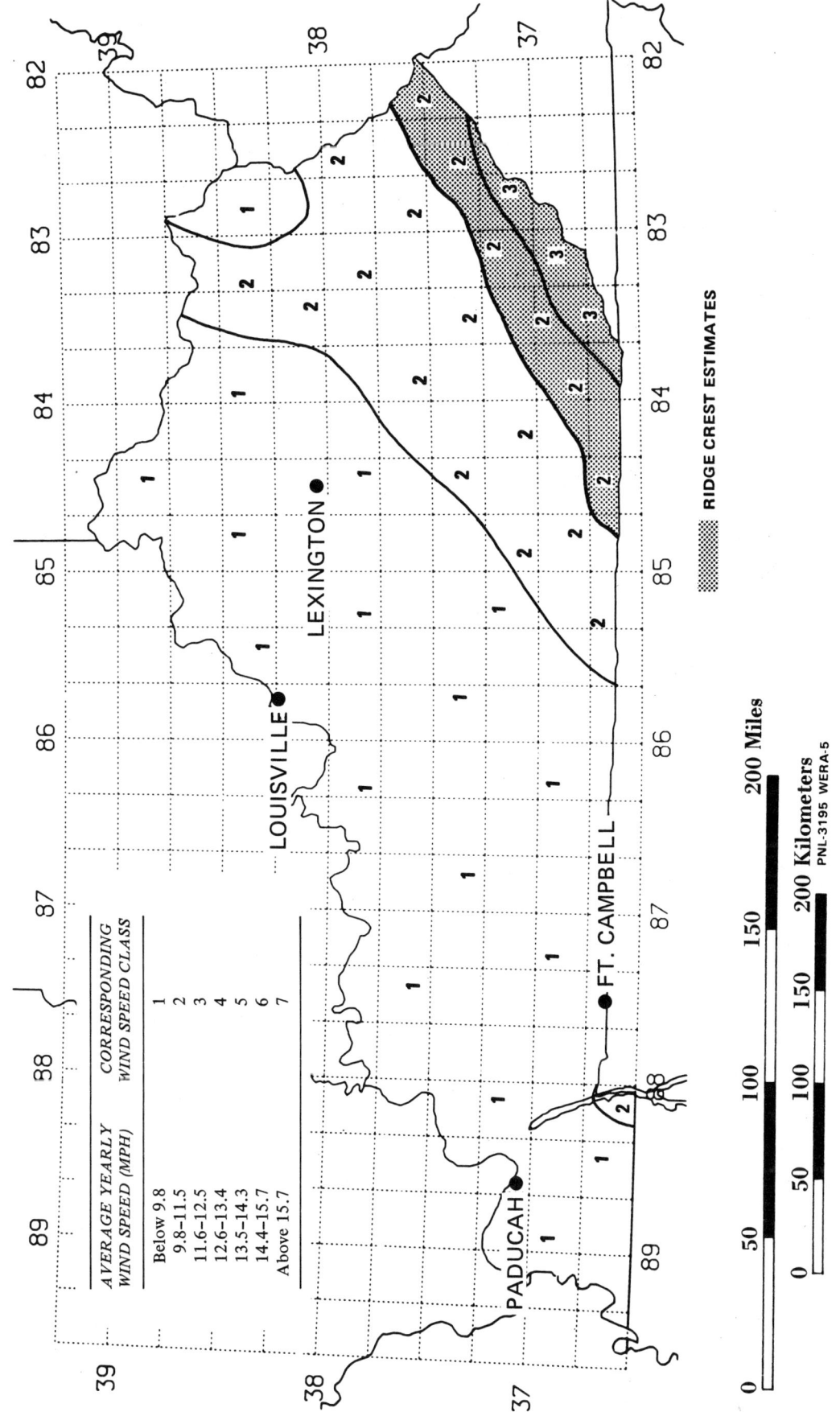

Fig. 20 Yearly average wind speeds in Kentucky.

38 SOUTH AND SOUTHEAST WIND ATLAS

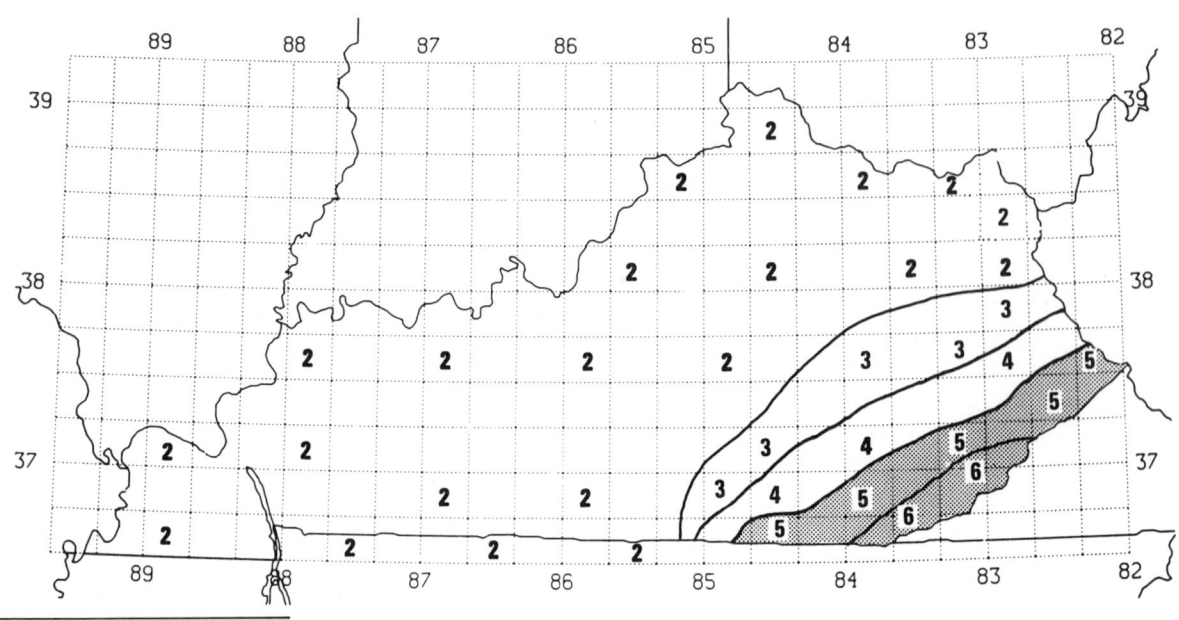

AVERAGE YEARLY WIND SPEED (MPH)	CORRESPONDING WIND SPEED CLASS
Below 9.8	1
9.8–11.5	2
11.6–12.5	3
12.6–13.4	4
13.5–14.3	5
14.4–15.7	6
Above 15.7	7

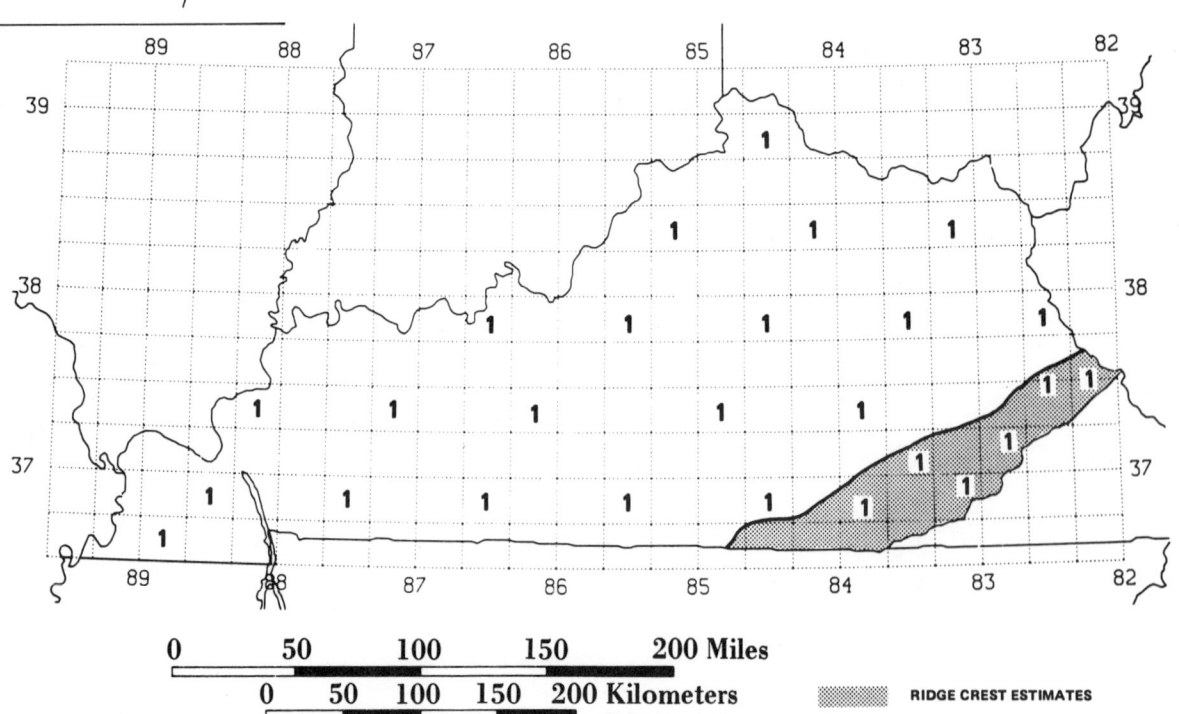

Fig. 21 Seasonal average wind speeds in Kentucky.

SPRING

RIDGE CREST ESTIMATES

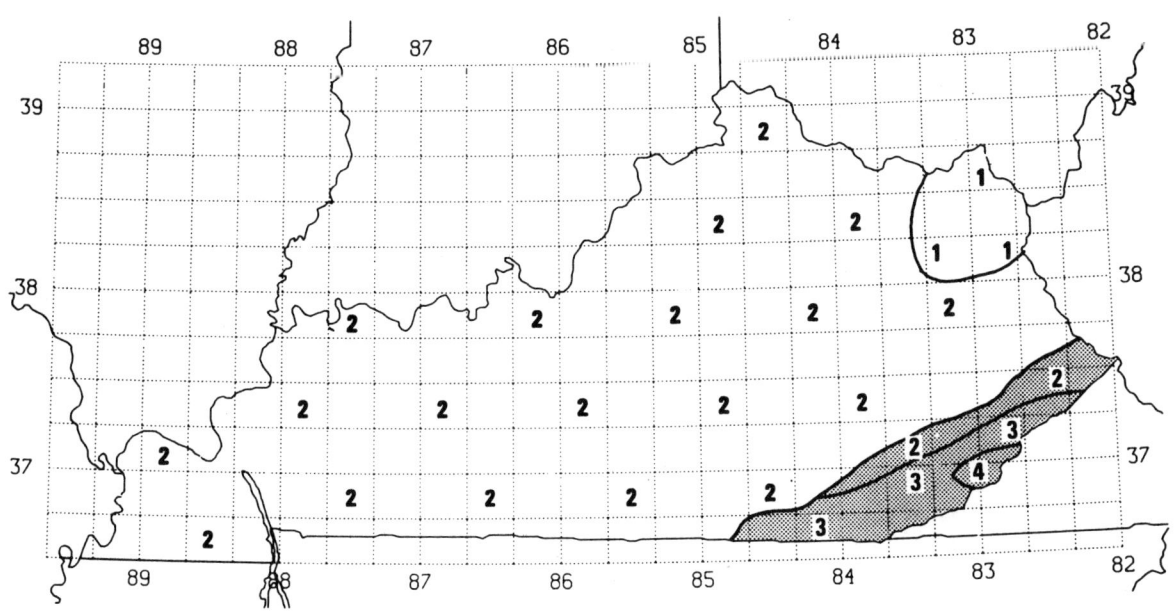

AVERAGE YEARLY WIND SPEED (MPH)	*CORRESPONDING WIND SPEED CLASS*
Below 9.8	1
9.8–11.5	2
11.6–12.5	3
12.6–13.4	4
13.5–14.3	5
14.4–15.7	6
Above 15.7	7

AUTUMN

0 50 100 150 200 Miles

0 50 100 150 200 Kilometers

PNL-3195 WERA-5

RIDGE CREST ESTIMATES

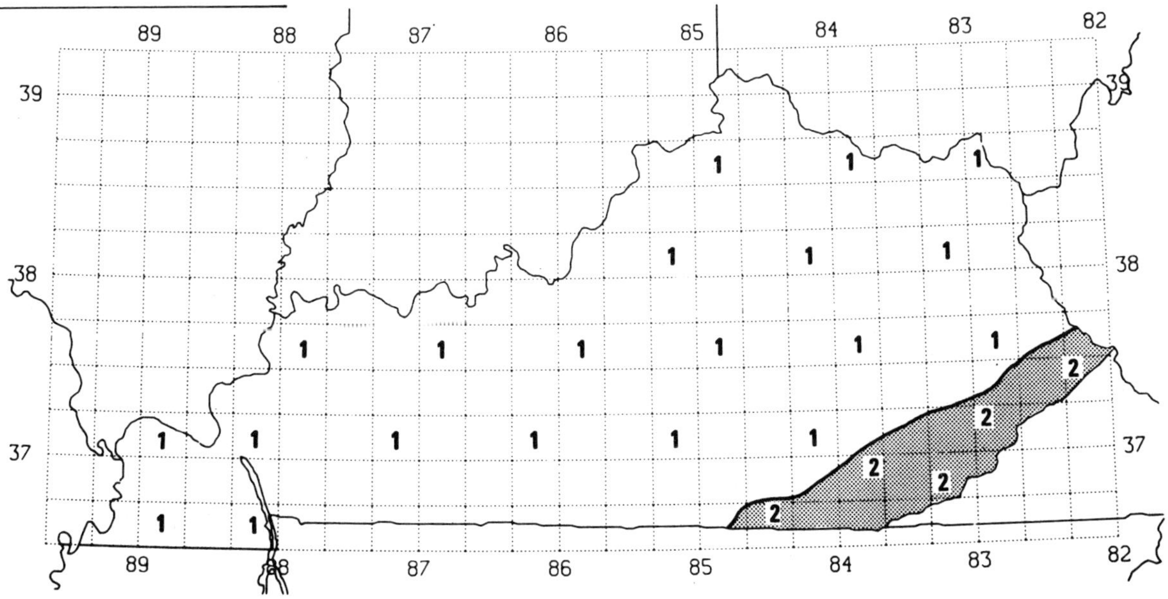

Fig. 22 Seasonal average wind speeds in Kentucky.

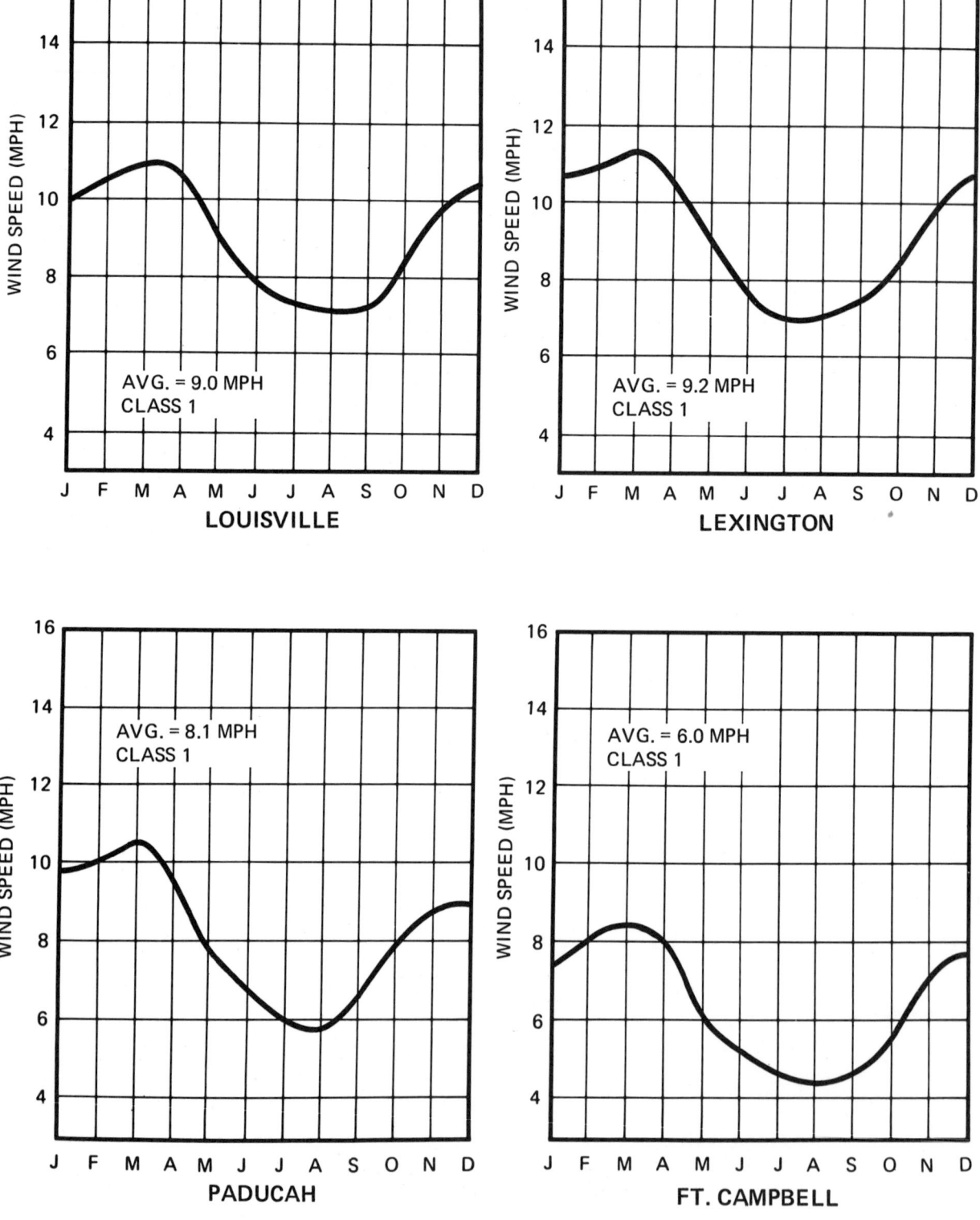

Fig. 23 Monthly average wind speeds in Kentucky.

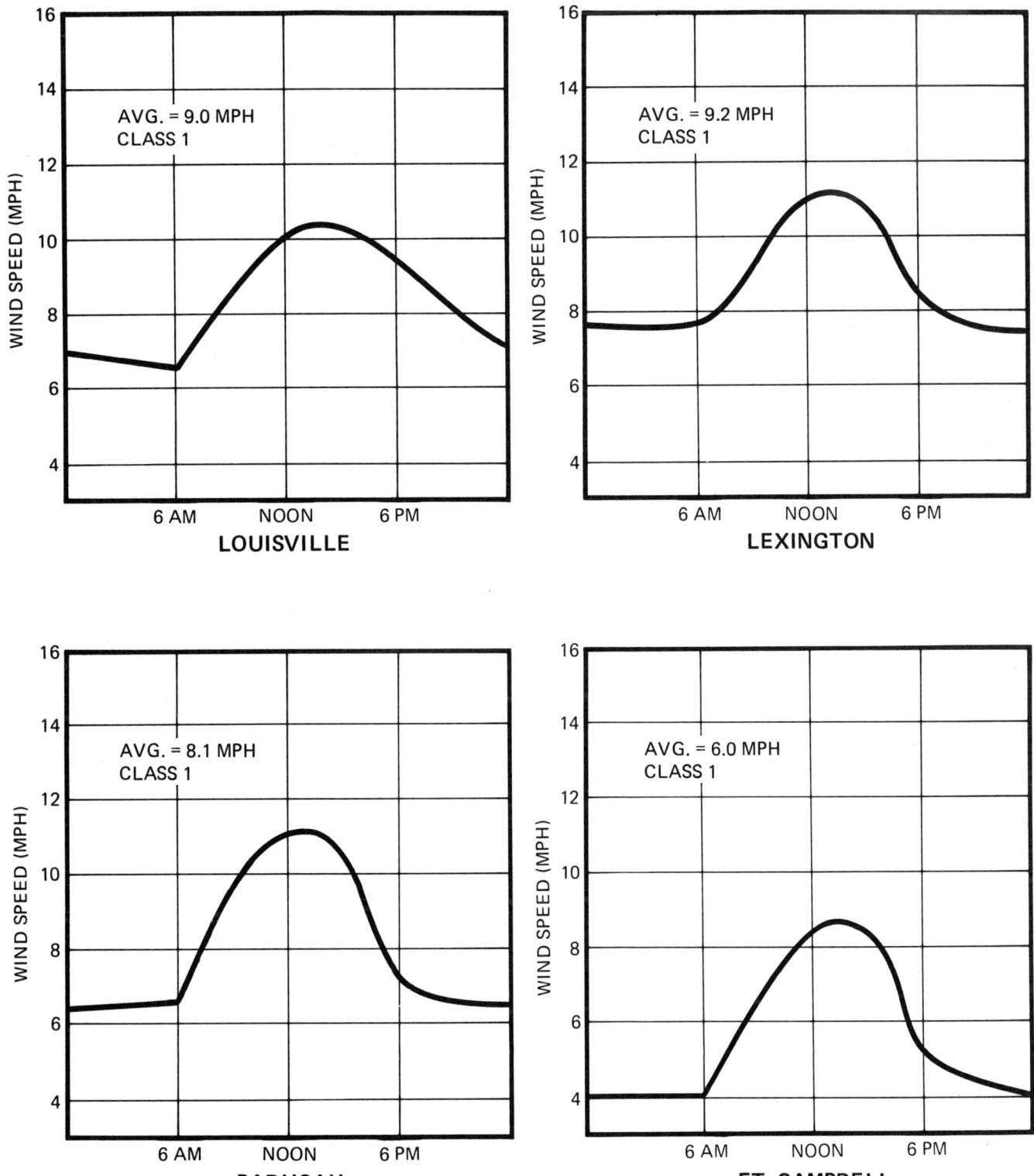

Fig. 24 Hourly average wind speeds in Kentucky.

TENNESSEE

YEARLY AVERAGE WIND SPEEDS

Some portions of Tennessee are marginally favorable for production of energy by wind power. Unfortunately, the strongest wind speeds occur only on the highest mountain ridges and fail to exceed Class 1 (more than 9.8 mph) in the vicinity of the major population centers where they could be best put to use. A map of yearly average wind speeds across the state is given in Fig. 25. Winds are as strong as Class 6 atop the highest peaks of the Great Smoky Mountains on the North Carolina border but no more than Class 2 to Class 3 over the ridges of the much lower Cumberland Plateau. In the Tennessee Valley, which separates the two mountain ranges, only Class 1 winds are found because the mountains block the free flow of the air. Winds are also Class 1 on the lower slopes and in the valleys of the mountainous areas.

In central and eastern Tennessee, winds reach Class 2 over exposed hilltops in the area adjacent to the Cumberland Plateau and also over the part of the Tennessee River Valley west of Nashville. Other jigsaw portions of eastern and central Tennessee, both to the north and south, are restricted to Class 1 winds, as is the entire western part of the state.

SEASONAL AVERAGE WIND SPEEDS

Average wind speeds during winter and summer in Tennessee are shown in Fig. 26, and during spring and autumn in Fig. 27. Winter and spring are the windiest seasons, with winter winds atop the mountain ridges being one to two classes stronger than springtime winds. At lower elevations, winter and spring winds average Class 1 in the Tennessee Valley and Class 2 over the central and western parts of the state.

Summer is a season of light winds as a rule, notwithstanding an occasional gusty thunderstorm, being Class 1 over the entire state except for a tiny patch of mountainous terrain in the extreme northeast, bordering on Virginia. Autumn winds are a little stronger. In the Appalachians, Class 2 winds occur on ridge crests and Class 3 to Class 4 winds atop the highest summits, but nonmountainous parts of the state continue to experience only Class 1 winds.

Monthly average wind speeds are shown in Fig. 28 at four Tennessee locations: Memphis and Nashville, which are both located in level or gently rolling terrain, and Bristol and Chattanooga, both sited in mountain valleys. Over the level terrain of the former cities, wind speeds are nearly Class 2, whereas in the valleys of the latter, the blocking effect of the mountains results in winds that average 3 to 4 mph lower. March is the month of strongest winds and August is the least windy month at all four locations.

AVERAGE WIND SPEEDS BY DAY AND NIGHT

Winds are strongest in Tennessee during early afternoon and lightest from about midnight till dawn. The difference between midnight and midday is greatest on sunny days, during spring and summer, and within mountain valleys. The hour-by-hour change in average wind speed at Memphis, Nashville, Bristol and Chattanooga is shown in Fig. 29. At Nashville and Memphis, the difference between the strongest winds in early afternoon and the lighter nighttime winds is about 3 to 4 mph. However, in the deeper mountain valleys, typified by Bristol and Chattanooga, winds are not only generally lighter than they are in more level regions, but nighttime winds are about 5 mph lighter than the peak winds that occur during the early afternoon.

44 SOUTH AND SOUTHEAST WIND ATLAS

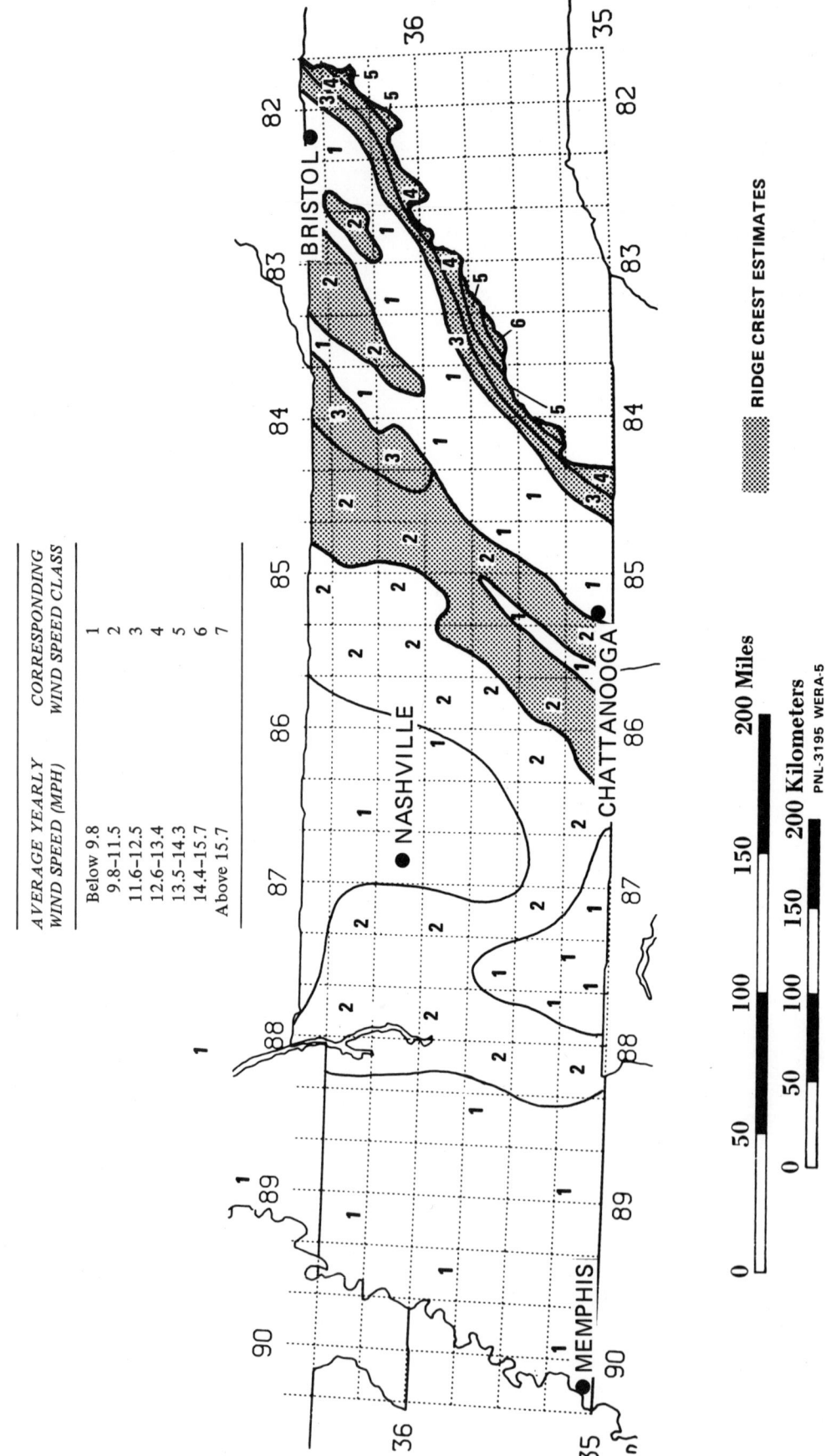

Fig. 25 Yearly average wind speeds in Tennessee.

TENNESSEE 45

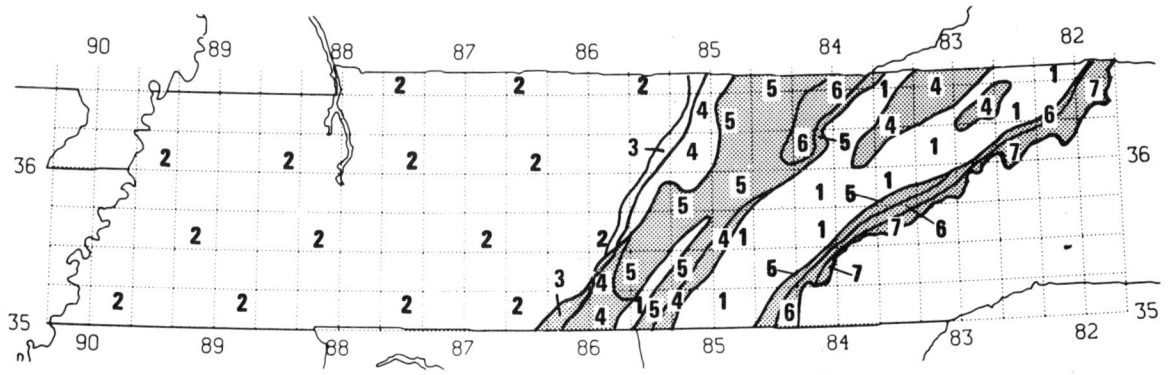

AVERAGE YEARLY WIND SPEED (MPH)	CORRESPONDING WIND SPEED CLASS
Below 9.8	1
9.8–11.5	2
11.6–12.5	3
12.6–13.4	4
13.5–14.3	5
14.4–15.7	6
Above 15.7	7

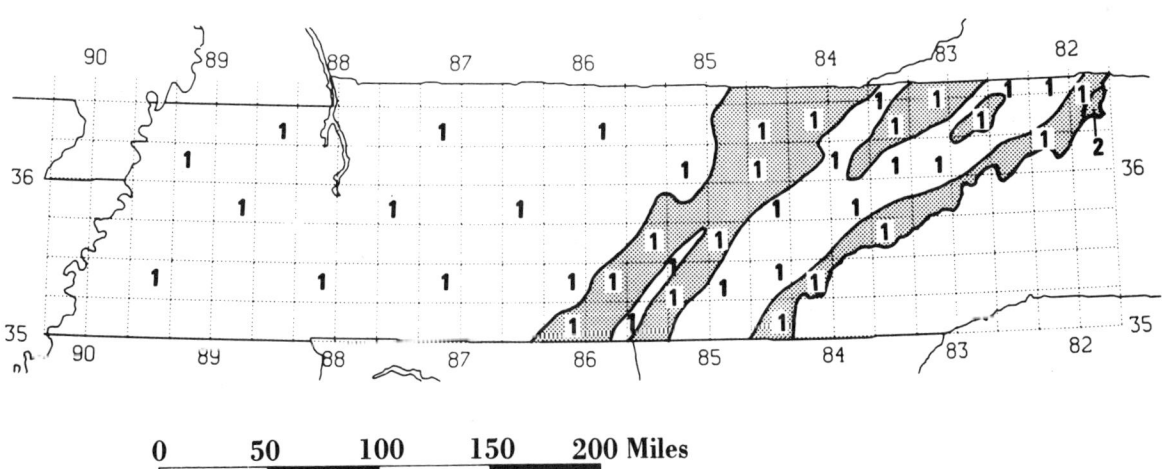

Fig. 26 Seasonal average wind speeds in Tennessee.

46 SOUTH AND SOUTHEAST WIND ATLAS

SPRING

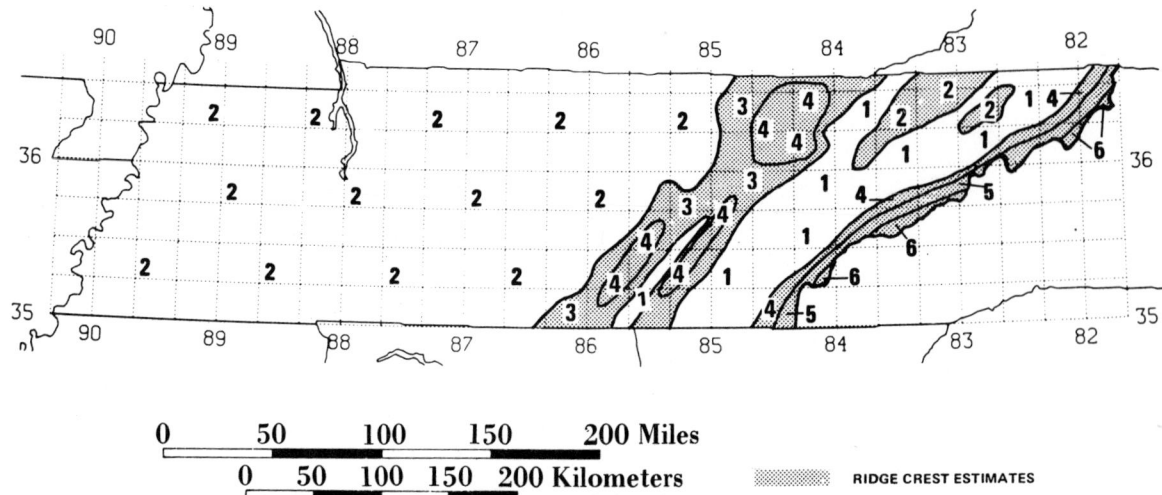

AVERAGE YEARLY WIND SPEED (MPH)	CORRESPONDING WIND SPEED CLASS
Below 9.8	1
9.8–11.5	2
11.6–12.5	3
12.6–13.4	4
13.5–14.3	5
14.4–15.7	6
Above 15.7	7

AUTUMN

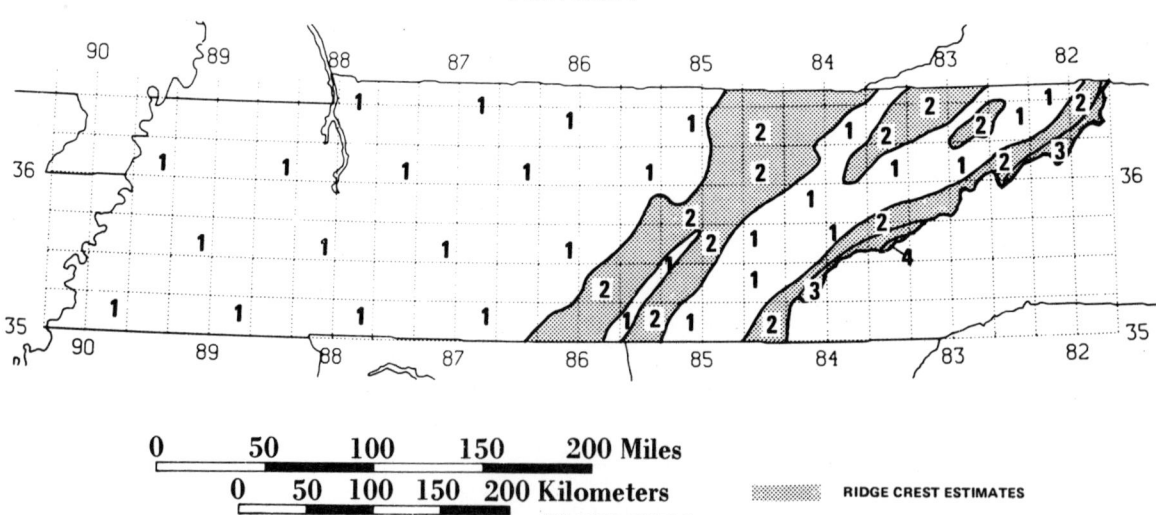

Fig. 27 Seasonal average wind speeds in Tennessee.

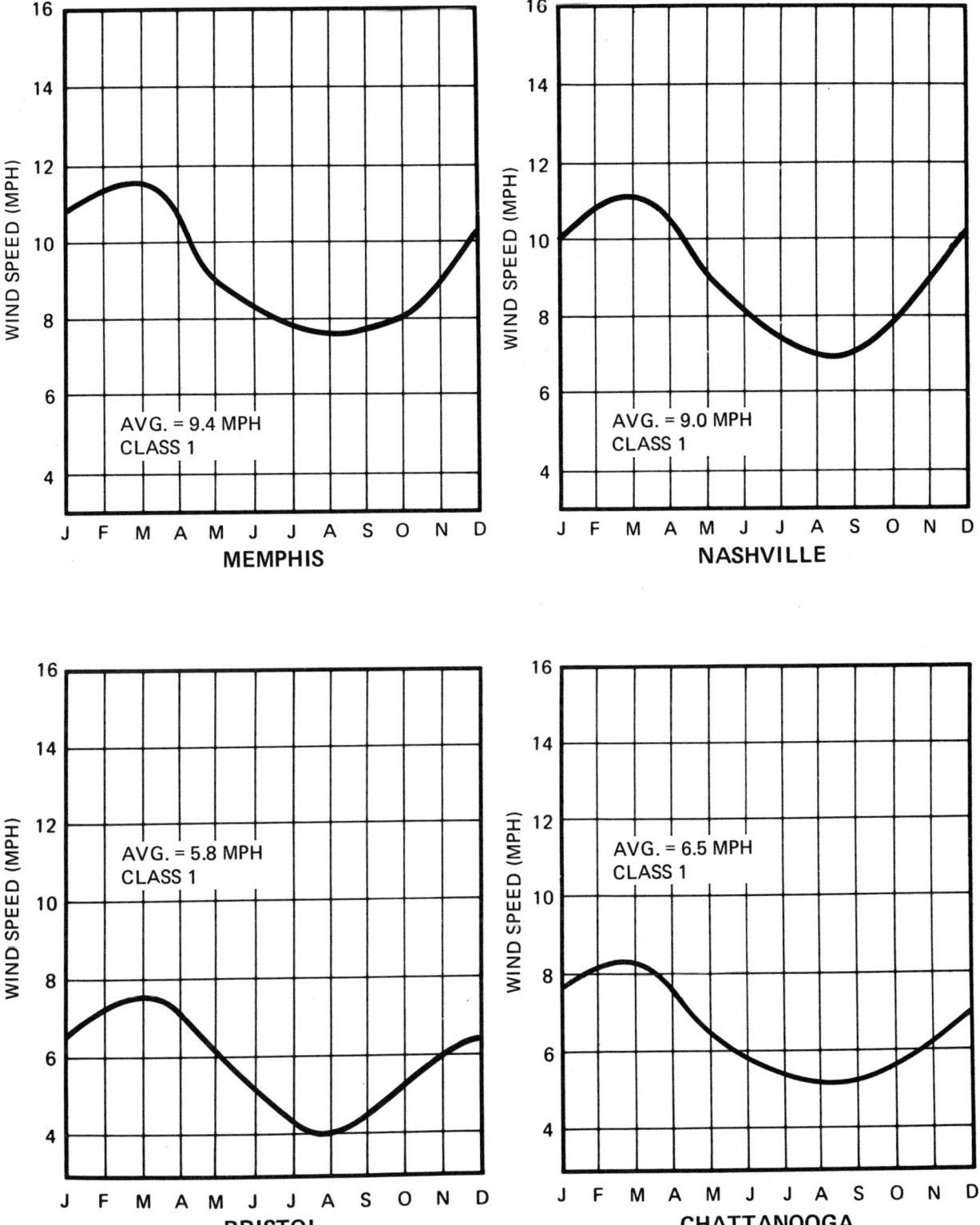

Fig. 28 Monthly average wind speeds in Tennessee.

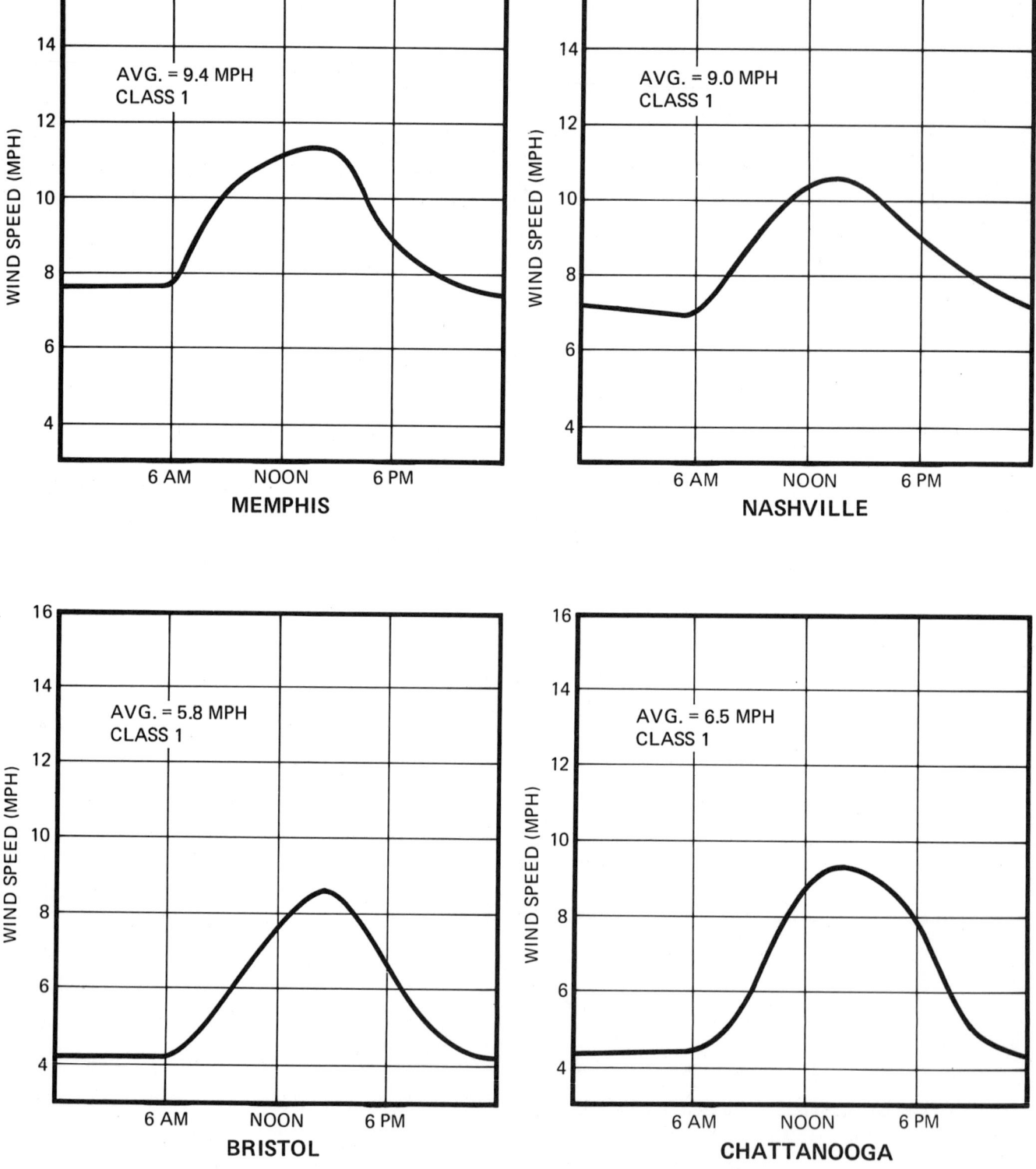

Fig. 29 Hourly average wind speeds in Tennessee.

WEST VIRGINIA

YEARLY AVERAGE WIND SPEEDS

Many good wind machine sites can be found among West Virginia's hills and mountains. The yearly average wind speeds for the state are shown in Fig. 30. Rough terrain is the essence of West Virginia, from the 4000-ft mountains in the east to the much lower, but equally numerous, hills in the west. Atop the ridge crests of the Appalachian and Allegheny Mountains (shaded areas in Fig. 30), average winds range from Class 2 to Class 5 (9.8 to 14.3 mph), with the higher winds on the highest of the ridges. Since the mountain valleys, whether narrow or broad, are sheltered from the stronger winds, they experience mainly Class 1 winds.

Unsheltered areas in the central and western parts of the state experience moderate (Class 2 to Class 3) winds, and there are many more wind machine sites among the broad uplands than on the narrow mountain ridges. Class 1 winds are the rule near the Ohio River. The desirability of a wind machine site is enhanced in any part of the state if a large, cleared area is available; forests and woods reduce wind speeds, even several hundred feet down wind.

SEASONAL AVERAGE WIND SPEEDS

West Virginia winds rise and fall with the march of the seasons. Average wind speeds for winter and summer are shown in Fig. 31 and for spring and autumn in Fig. 32.

Winter is decidedly the windiest season. Ridge crest speeds are in the Class 7 range over a broad area of the eastern part of the state. The central uplands experience Class 4 to Class 5 winds, and even the Ohio River Valley has Class 2 winds. Spring winds are two to three classes lower than winter winds over the mountains and uplands and one to two classes lower over the lower elevations in the west. Summer brings only the gentlest of breezes, all regions of the state being Class 1 except for the highest mountaintops, which are Class 2. In autumn, winds are one to two classes stronger than in summer, except that the western third of the state remains becalmed at Class 1.

Average monthly wind speeds at Charleston, Martinsburg (within an eastern panhandle valley), Wheeling, and Huntington are shown in Fig. 33. All four of these locations average only Class 1 winds, a consequence of their being sited either near the Ohio River Valley (Wheeling and Huntington) or in valleys in mountainous or hilly terrain (Charleston and Martinsburg). Only in Wheeling in winter do winds average Class 2.

March is the windiest, and August the calmest, month at all four locations. The difference between March and August wind speeds ranges from 3 mph at Charleston to 5 mph at Wheeling.

AVERAGE WIND SPEEDS BY DAY AND NIGHT

The change in West Virginia average wind speeds from day to night is similar to that in other East Central states. Winds increase rapidly after sunrise to an early afternoon peak that is followed by a rapid decrease until late evening and stable, relatively light winds through the night.

Wind speeds over the course of the 24-hour cycle are shown for Charleston, Martinsburg, Wheeling, and Huntington in Fig. 34. Peak speeds come in early afternoon, a bit earlier during winter than in summer. The largest difference between nighttime and daytime winds—5mph—is at Martinsburg, which is situated in a deep valley. Over the more open terrain at Wheeling, the difference is 3 mph.

The day-night change in windspeed atop mountain ridges where the best wind machine sites are to be found may be less than that in open terrain. In some cases, nighttime winds may actually exceed daytime winds.

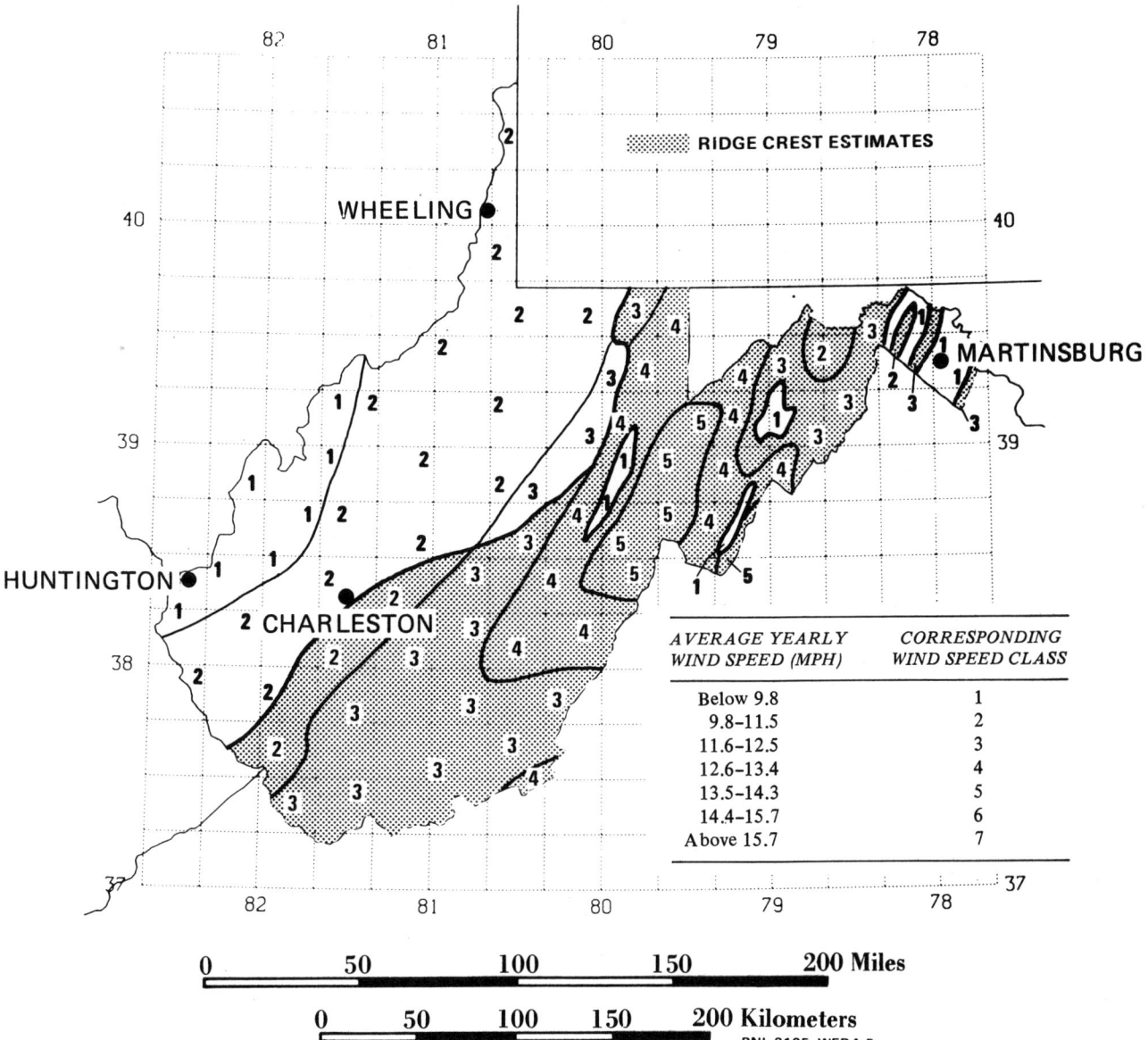

Fig. 30 Yearly average wind speeds in West Virginia.

52 SOUTH AND SOUTHEAST WIND ATLAS

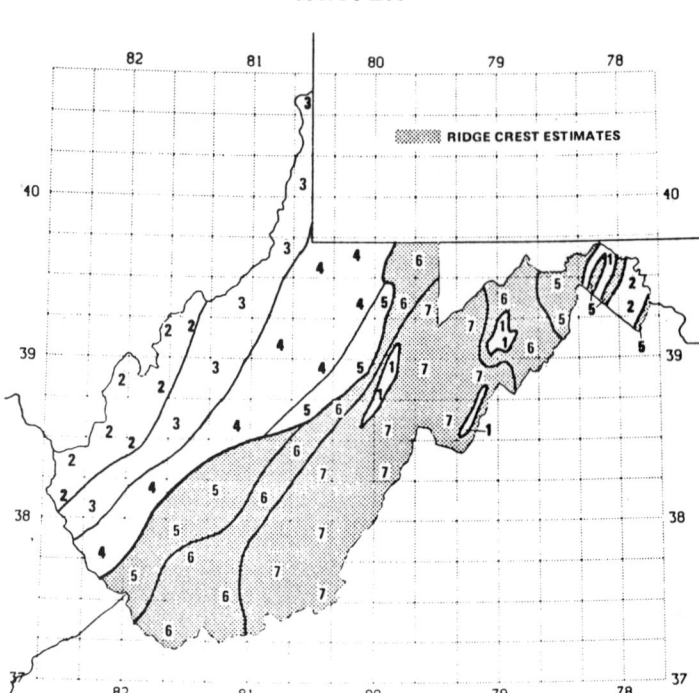

AVERAGE YEARLY WIND SPEED (MPH)	CORRESPONDING WIND SPEED CLASS
Below 9.8	1
9.8–11.5	2
11.6–12.5	3
12.6–13.4	4
13.5–14.3	5
14.4–15.7	6
Above 15.7	7

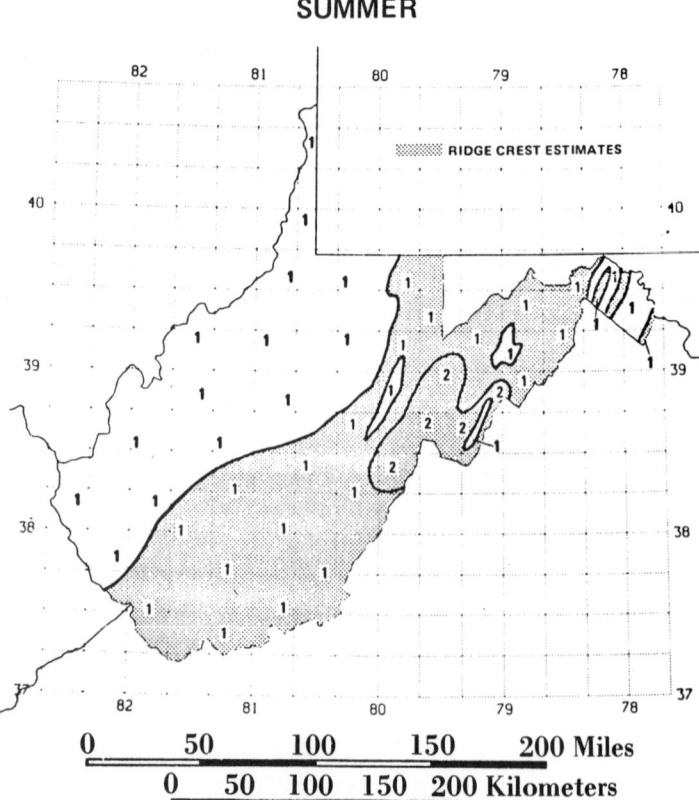

Fig. 31 Seasonal average wind speeds in West Virginia.

WEST VIRGINIA

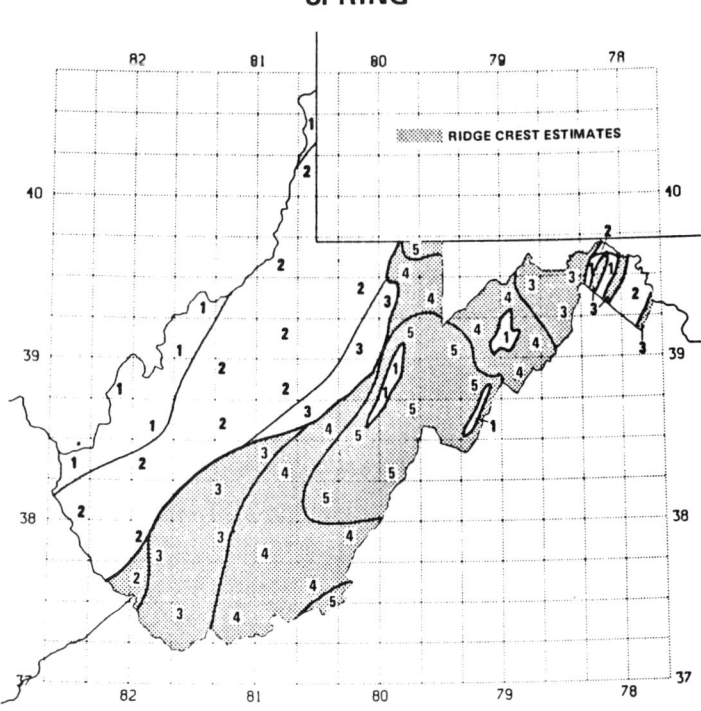

AVERAGE YEARLY WIND SPEED (MPH)	CORRESPONDING WIND SPEED CLASS
Below 9.8	1
9.8–11.5	2
11.6–12.5	3
12.6–13.4	4
13.5–14.3	5
14.4–15.7	6
Above 15.7	7

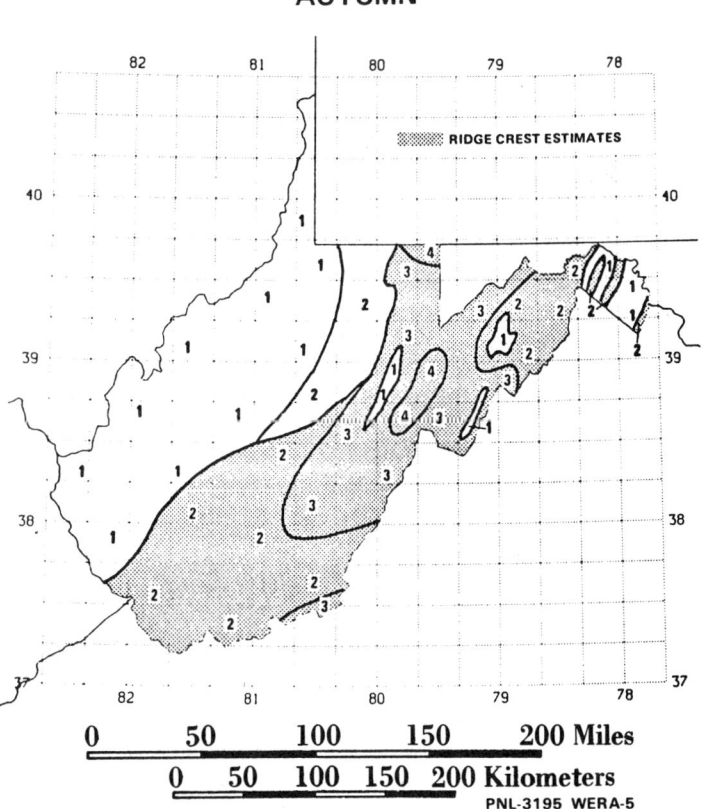

Fig. 32 Seasonal average wind speeds in West Virginia.

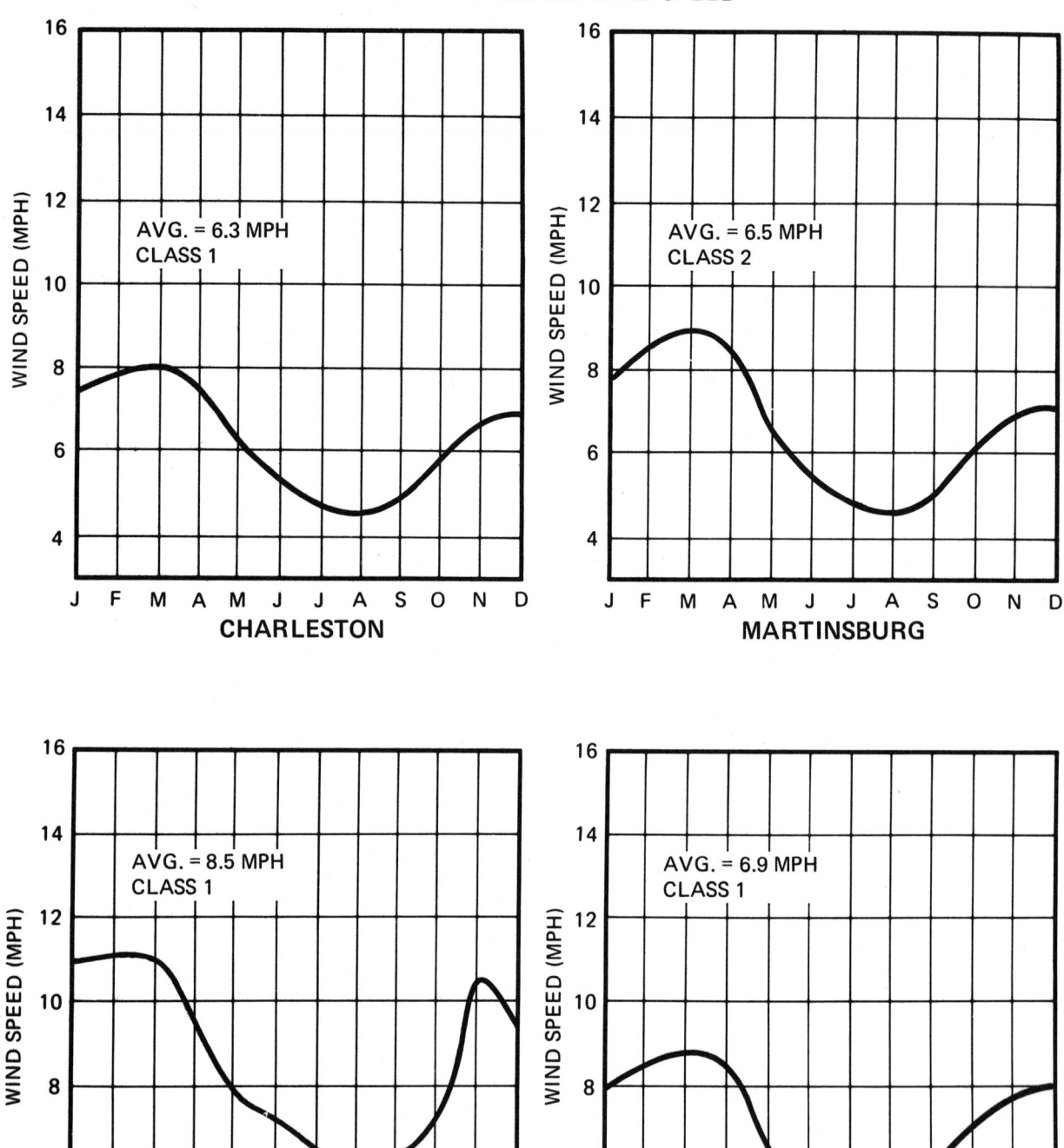

Fig. 33 Monthly average wind speeds in West Virginia.

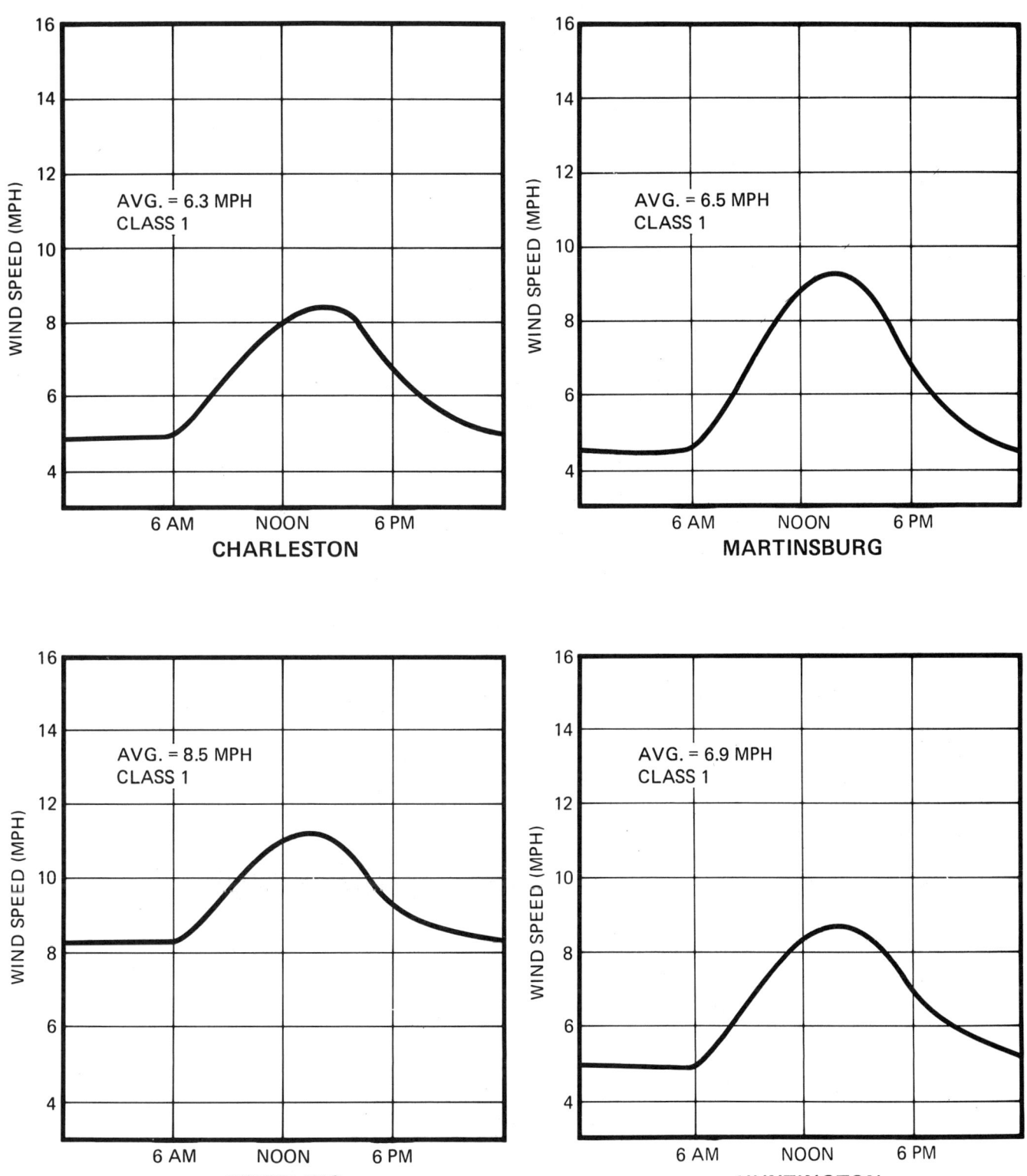

Fig. 34 Hourly average wind speeds in West Virginia.

MARYLAND – DELAWARE

YEARLY AVERAGE WIND SPEEDS

There are two portions of Maryland and one of Delaware that offer potential wind machine sites—in the former, atop the ridges of the Appalachian Mountains in the west and near the shores of Chesapeake Bay, and in the latter, along the Atlantic Ocean. In other areas, wind speeds are too low for profitable wind machine operation.

The location of the Appalachian Mountain ridges is shown by the shaded portions of the yearly average wind speed map of Maryland and Delaware in Fig. 35. Ridgetop windspeeds are Class 4 (12.5 to 13.4 mph) over the higher western ridges and Class 2 or 3 over the lower ridges farther east. In the valleys between the mountains and on the lower mountain slopes, winds subside to Class 1. Class 1 winds are also the rule over the remainder of the two states (including Washington, D.C.) except within 5 to 10 miles of the shores of Chesapeake Bay or the Atlantic Ocean. Well exposed coastal locations enjoy Class 3 winds, and Class 2 winds blow over points slightly inland.

SEASONAL AVERAGE WIND SPEEDS

Average wind speeds for winter and summer are shown in Fig. 36 and for spring and autumn in Fig. 37. During winter, winds range from Class 5 to Class 7—the strongest of the year—over the exposed ridges of the Appalachians. Coastal sites also experience the strongest winds, as high as Class 5 at the most exposed points and Class 3 to Class 4 over most islands and peninsulas. The remainder of Maryland and Delaware experience Class 2 wind speeds.

Springtime wind speeds are strongest in March and decrease rather rapidly in April and May. Average spring speeds are Class 3 to 5 over well-exposed mountain terrain and Class 3 over the great majority of coastal areas. Summer and autumn are the seasons of lowest wind speeds; autumnal winds are significantly stronger than summer winds over the mountain ridges and only slightly stronger at coastal locations.

Monthly average wind speeds are shown for Wilmington, Delaware, and Salisbury, Baltimore, and Patuxent River, Maryland, in Fig. 38. The strongest winds blow during March (except April at Patuxent River), and August is the stillest month. The difference between the windiest and stillest months amounts to 4 mph at Wilmington and 3 mph at the other locations.

AVERAGE WIND SPEEDS BY DAY AND NIGHT

Winds in Maryland and Delaware are significantly stronger during the day than at night. The change in average wind speed over the daily cycle at Wilmington, Salisbury, Baltimore, and Patuxent River is shown in Fig. 39. Winds are usually at their strongest in early afternoon and at their lightest from about midnight to sunrise. The difference is greatest—6 mph—at Salisbury and least—3 mph—at Patuxent River.

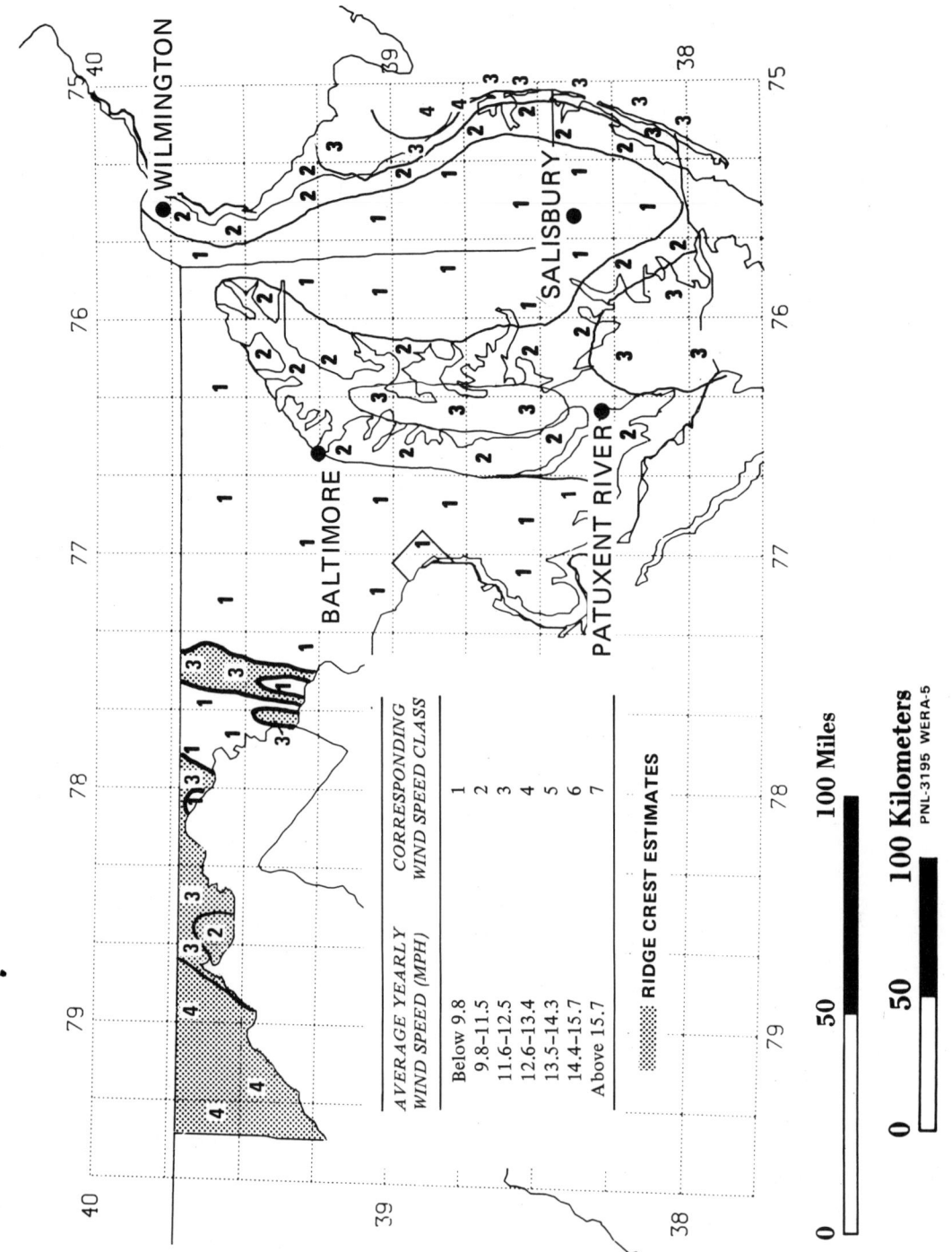

Fig. 35 Yearly average wind speeds in Maryland-Delaware.

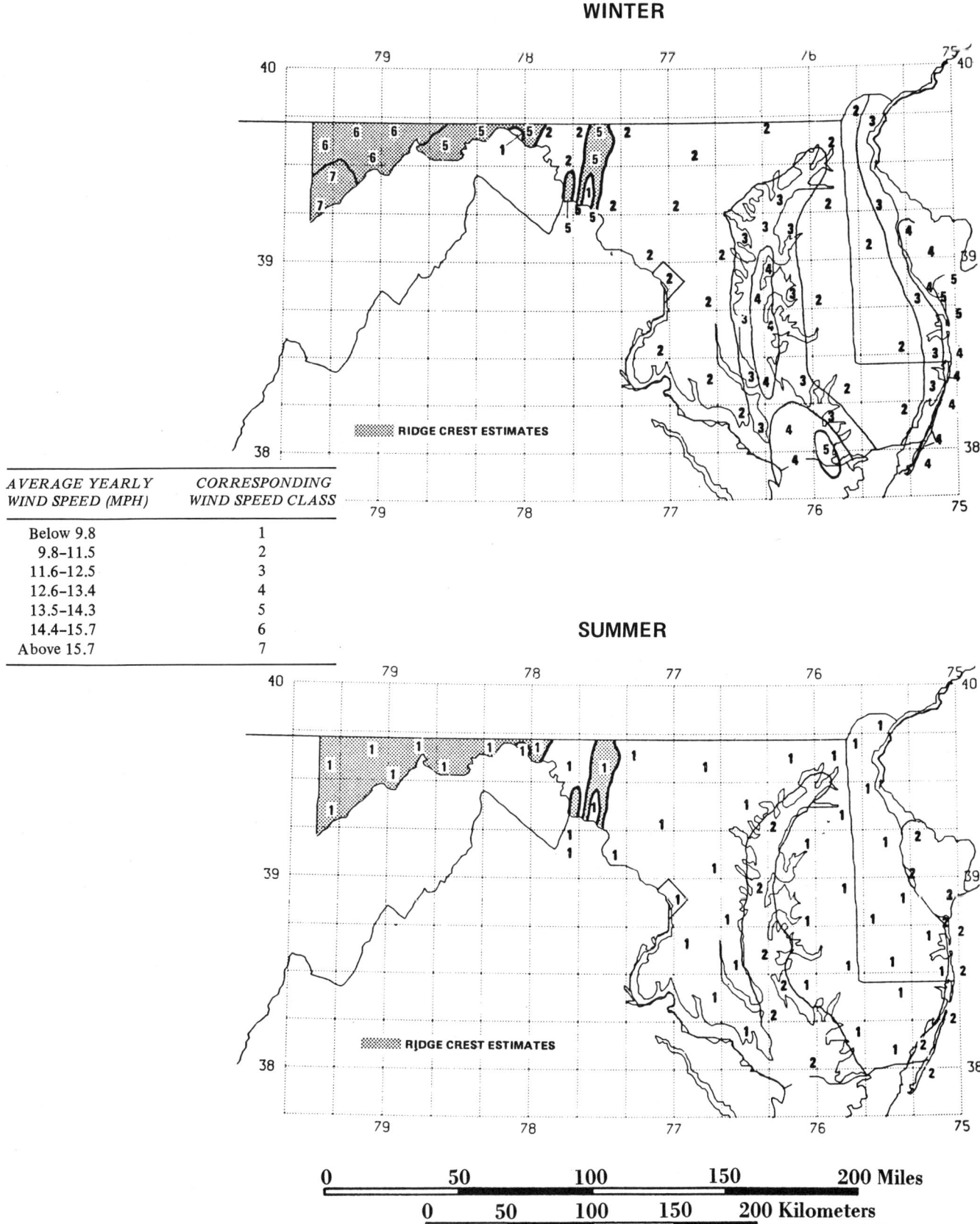

AVERAGE YEARLY WIND SPEED (MPH)	CORRESPONDING WIND SPEED CLASS
Below 9.8	1
9.8–11.5	2
11.6–12.5	3
12.6–13.4	4
13.5–14.3	5
14.4–15.7	6
Above 15.7	7

Fig. 36 Seasonal average wind speeds in Maryland-Delaware.

60 SOUTH AND SOUTHEAST WIND ATLAS

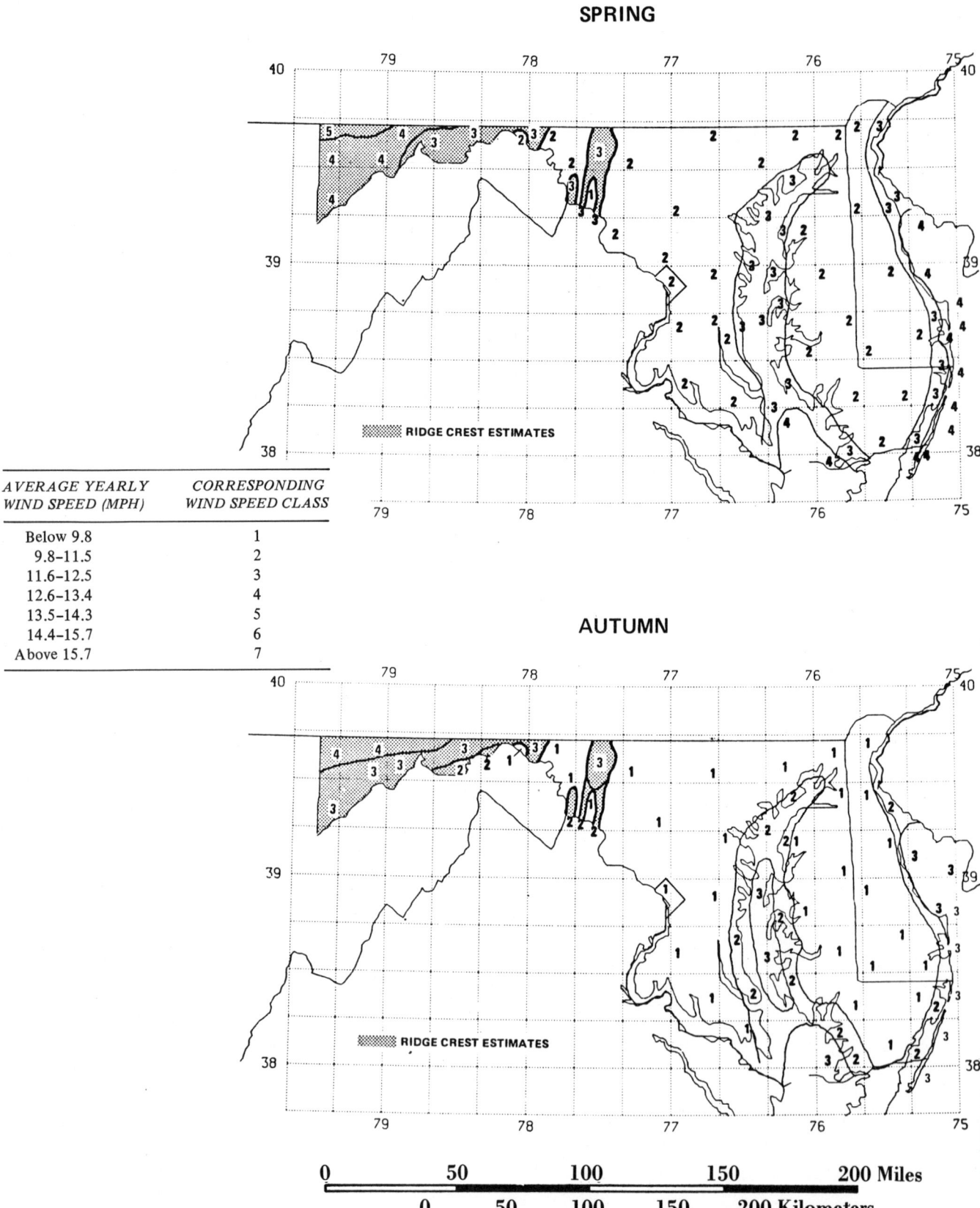

AVERAGE YEARLY WIND SPEED (MPH)	CORRESPONDING WIND SPEED CLASS
Below 9.8	1
9.8–11.5	2
11.6–12.5	3
12.6–13.4	4
13.5–14.3	5
14.4–15.7	6
Above 15.7	7

Fig. 37 Seasonal average wind speeds in Maryland-Delaware.

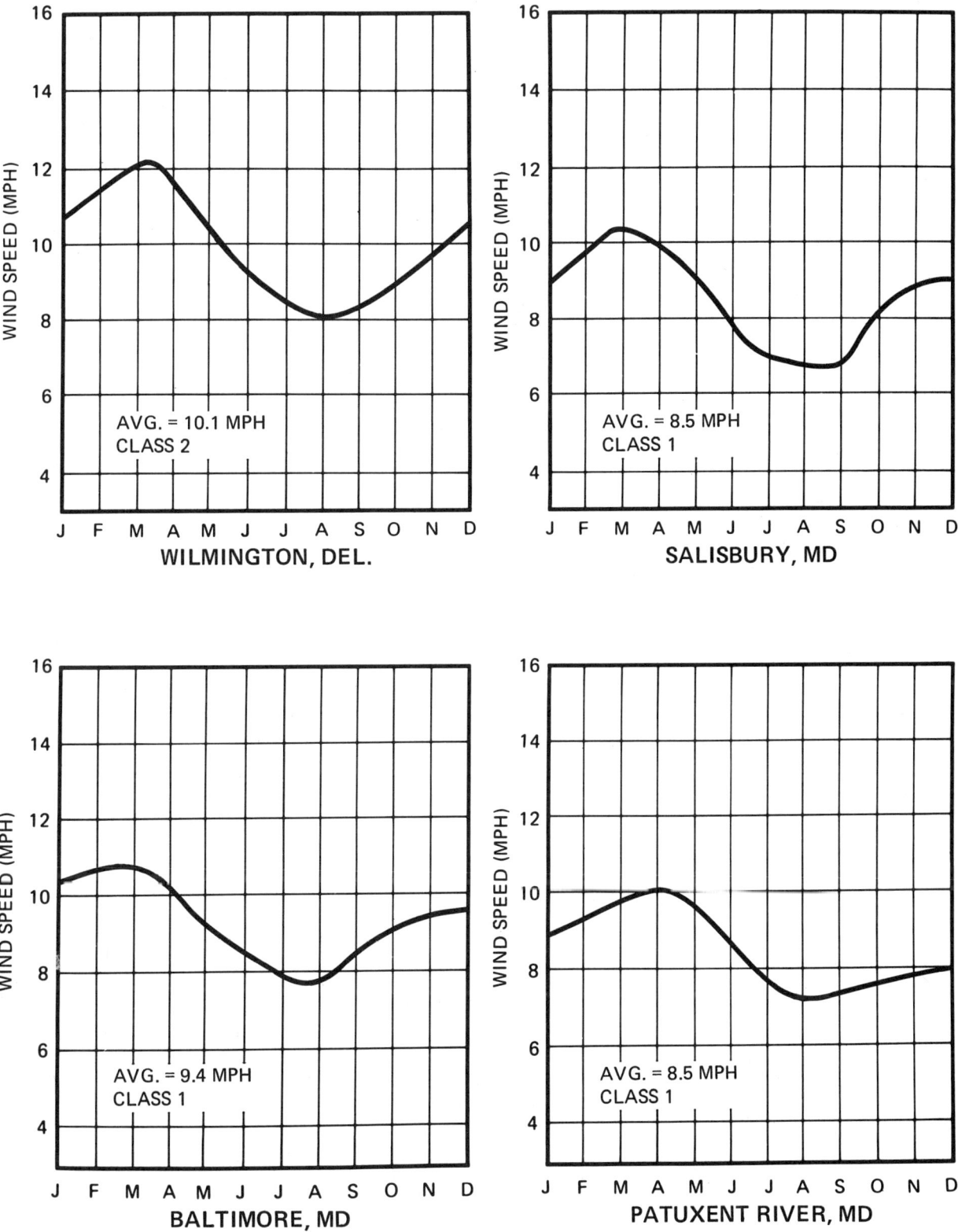

Fig. 38 Monthly average wind speeds in Maryland-Delaware.

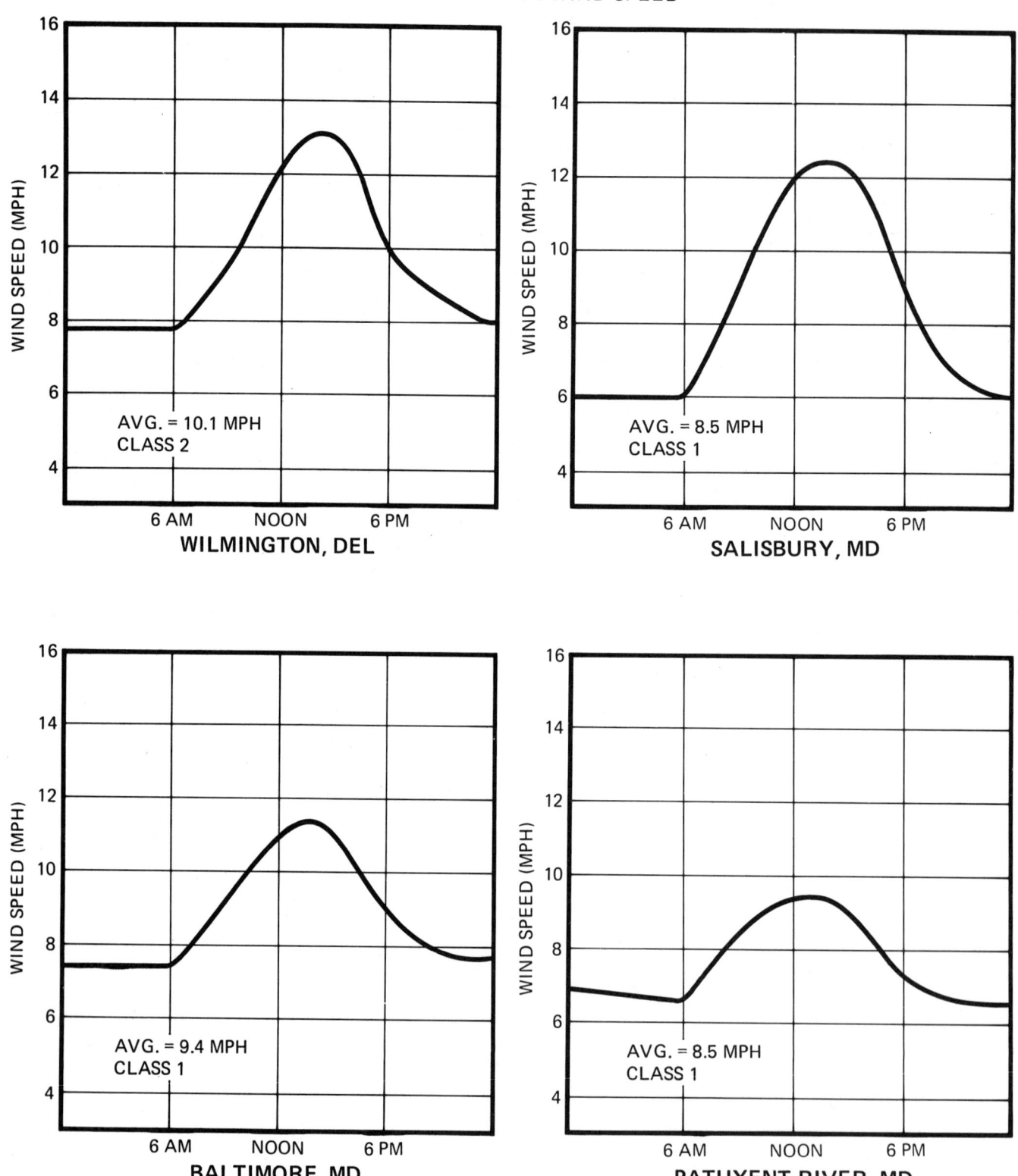

Fig. 39 Hourly average wind speeds in Maryland-Delaware.

VIRGINIA

YEARLY AVERAGE WIND SPEEDS

Wind speeds over most of Virginia are quite light; however, on the ridge crests of the Appalachian Mountains in the northwest, and along the shores of the Atlantic Ocean and Chesapeake Bay, they may be high enough to warrant investment in a wind machine. As indicated by Fig. 40, yearly average wind speeds reach Class 5 (13.4 to 14.3 mph) on the highest and most exposed mountain ridges; unfortunately, these are much less accessible than the more populous valleys between the mountains.

More promising are the Class 2 to Class 4 winds along the shores of Chesapeake Bay and the Atlantic Ocean. Coastal sites for wind machines are numerous because of the levelness of the land. Trees and buildings comprise the only obstacles to the free flow of wind. The best sites (Class 4) are found on the southernmost tip of the Delmarva Peninsula and the immediate Atlantic shore south of Norfolk. Exposed points along Chesapeake Bay enjoy Class 3 winds, and Class 2 winds extend here as much as 15 miles inland. The remainder of the state—including Washington, D.C. and the picturesque valleys of the far west—are limited to Class 1 winds.

SEASONAL AVERAGE WIND SPEEDS

The variability of average wind speeds over the seasons is shown in Fig. 41 for winter and summer and in Fig. 42 for spring and autumn. Winter winds are a fierce Class 7 atop the mountains bordering West Virginia and Class 6 on most of the lesser mountains. In the mountain valleys, they are only Class 1 or 2. Exposed coastal points enjoy Class 3 to Class 4 speeds, with Class 2 winds extending eastward as well as into the flat urbanized northern part of the state. Elsewhere, winds are typical of Dixie, that is, a disappointing Class 1.

Summer winds are inadequate everywhere in Virginia for the production of energy from the wind. Even the highest mountains and most exposed shores manage only Class 2 winds; 99 percent of the state is Class 1.

Average monthly wind speeds at Roanoke, Dulles Airport (just west of Washington, D.C.), Norfolk, and Richmond are shown in Fig. 43. Norfolk's Class 2 winds are typical of less exposed coastal points, and the remaining three locations—all of which have Class 1 winds—are typical of mountain valleys (in the case of Roanoke) or of level inland sites (Dulles Airport and Richmond). Wind speeds are highest in March and lowest in August at all four locations.

AVERAGE WIND SPEEDS BY DAY AND NIGHT

The change of wind speed by hour of the day in Virginia follows the typical pattern: strongest in early afternoon, decreasing until midnight, with a steady minimum until dawn and a rapid increase during the morning. This pattern is revealed by the average wind speeds shown in Fig. 44 for Roanoke, Dulles Airport, Norfolk, and Richmond. The difference between the peak and minimum speeds of the 24-hour cycle averages 4 to 5 mph; it is greatest in late spring and early summer and on days with abundant sunshine.

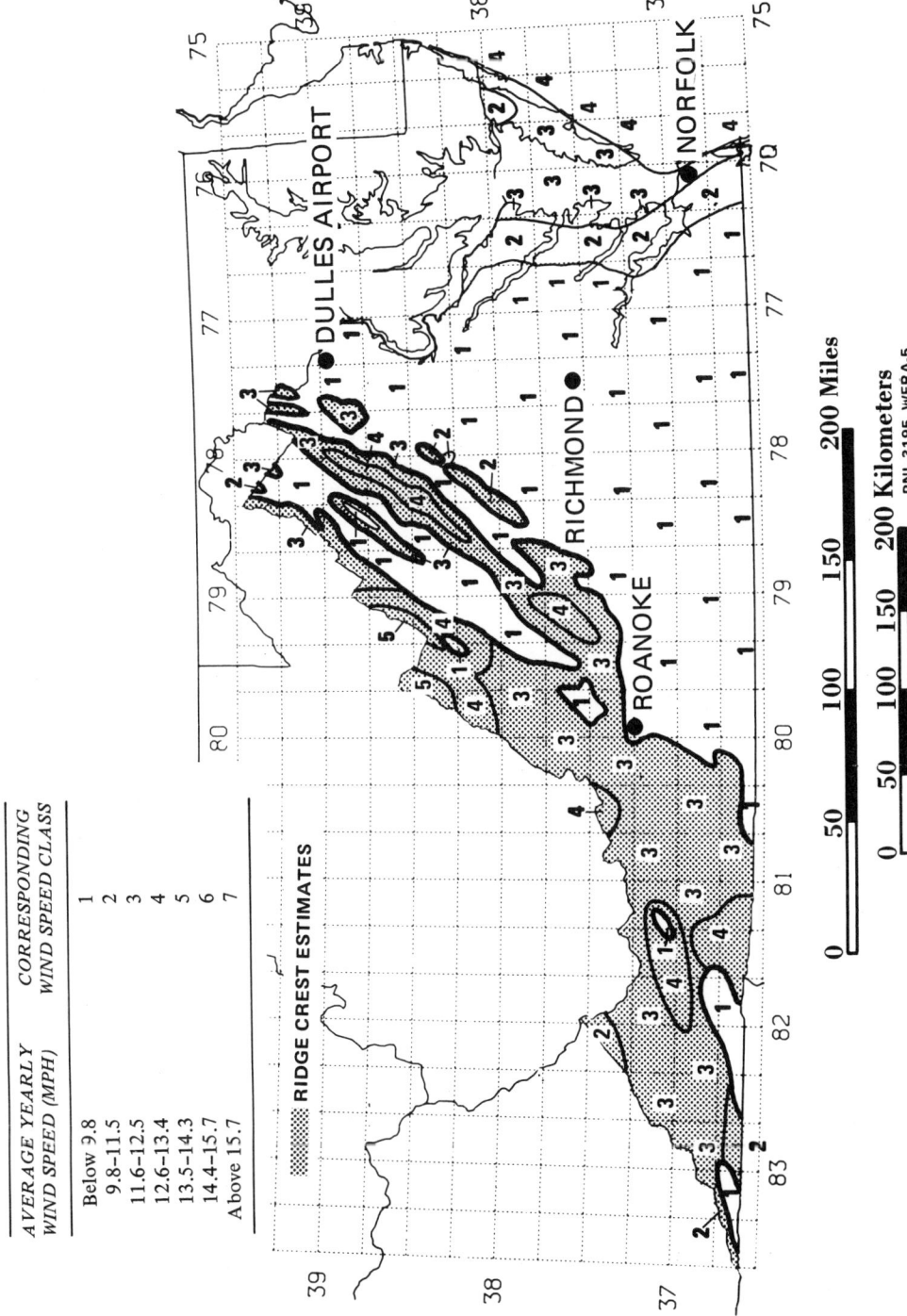

Fig. 40 Yearly average wind speeds in Virginia.

66 SOUTH AND SOUTHEAST WIND ATLAS

WINTER

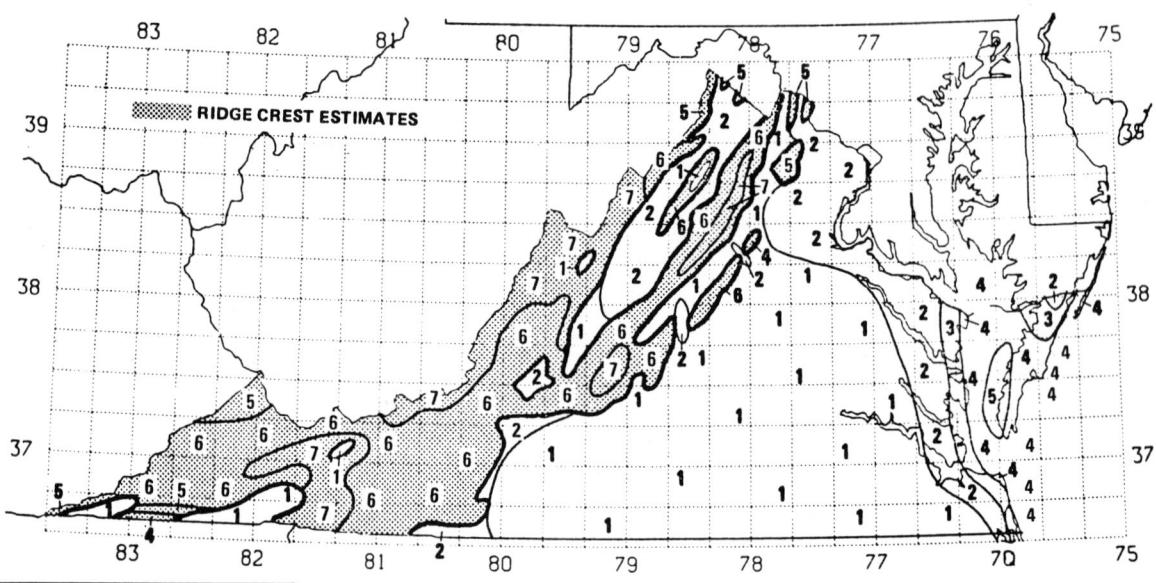

AVERAGE YEARLY WIND SPEED (MPH)	CORRESPONDING WIND SPEED CLASS
Below 9.8	1
9.8–11.5	2
11.6–12.5	3
12.6–13.4	4
13.5–14.3	5
14.4–15.7	6
Above 15.7	7

SUMMER

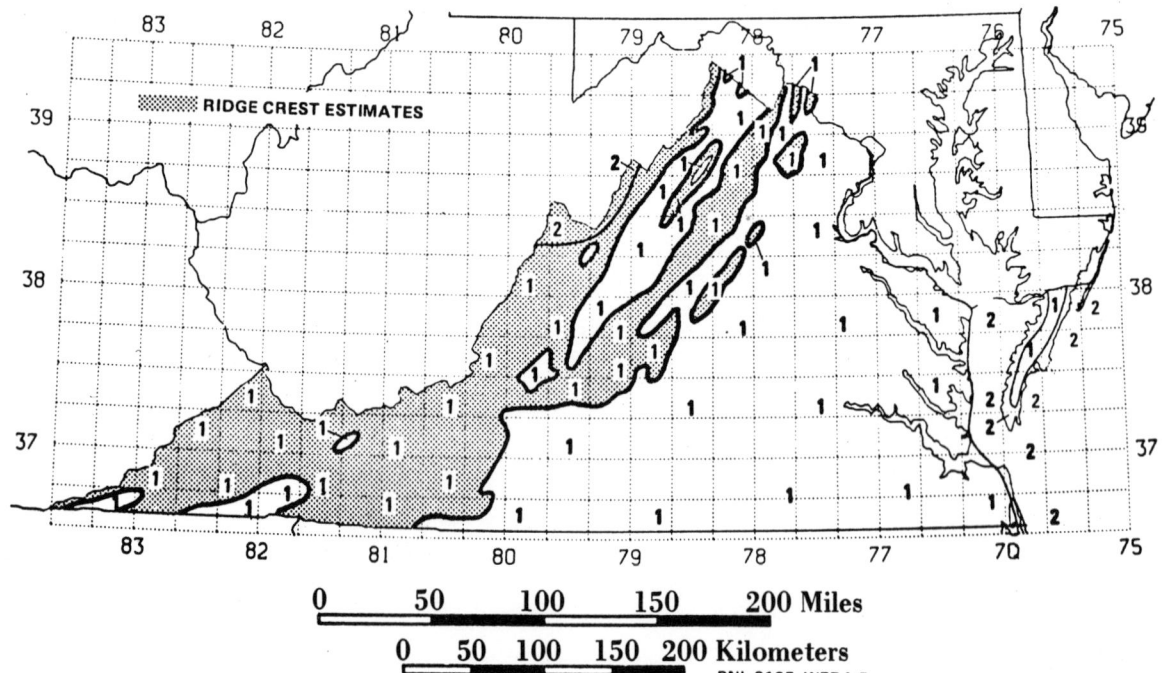

Fig. 41 Seasonal average wind speeds in Virginia.

SPRING

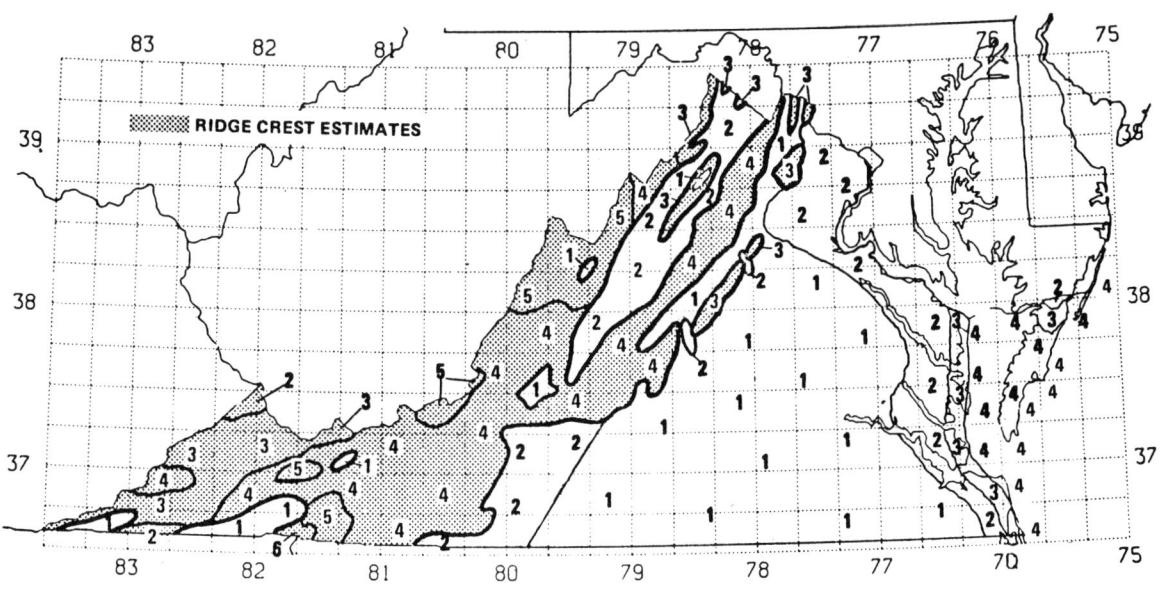

AVERAGE YEARLY WIND SPEED (MPH)	CORRESPONDING WIND SPEED CLASS
Below 9.8	1
9.8–11.5	2
11.6–12.5	3
12.6–13.4	4
13.5–14.3	5
14.4–15.7	6
Above 15.7	7

AUTUMN

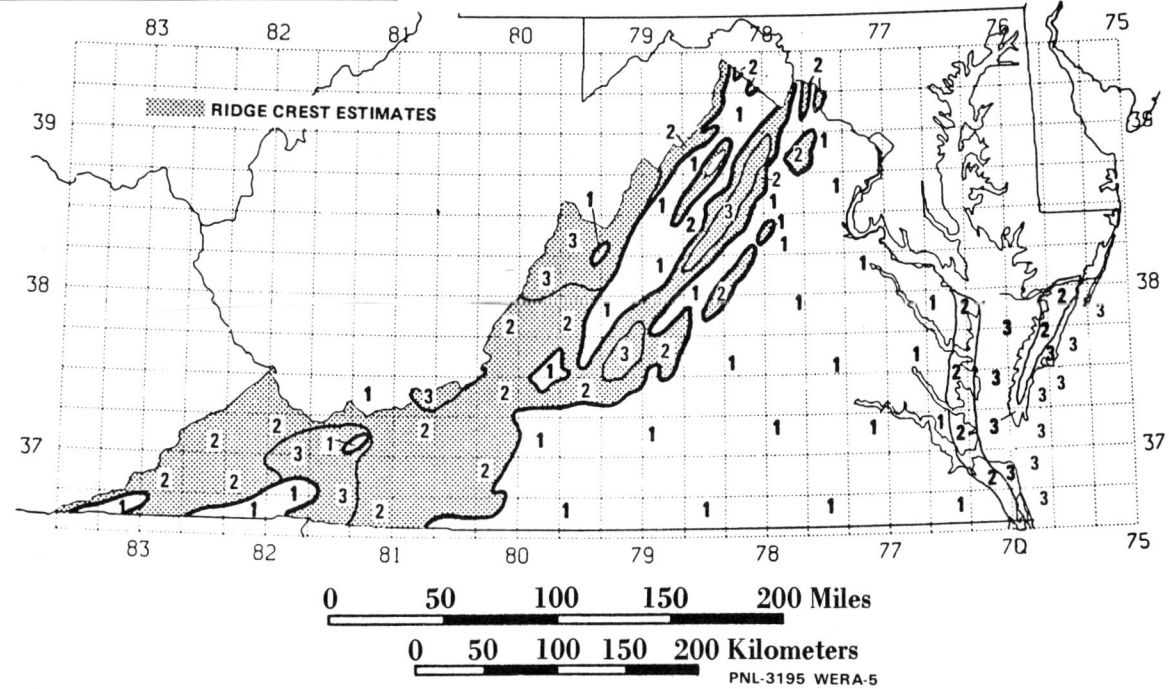

Fig. 42 Seasonal average wind speeds in Virginia.

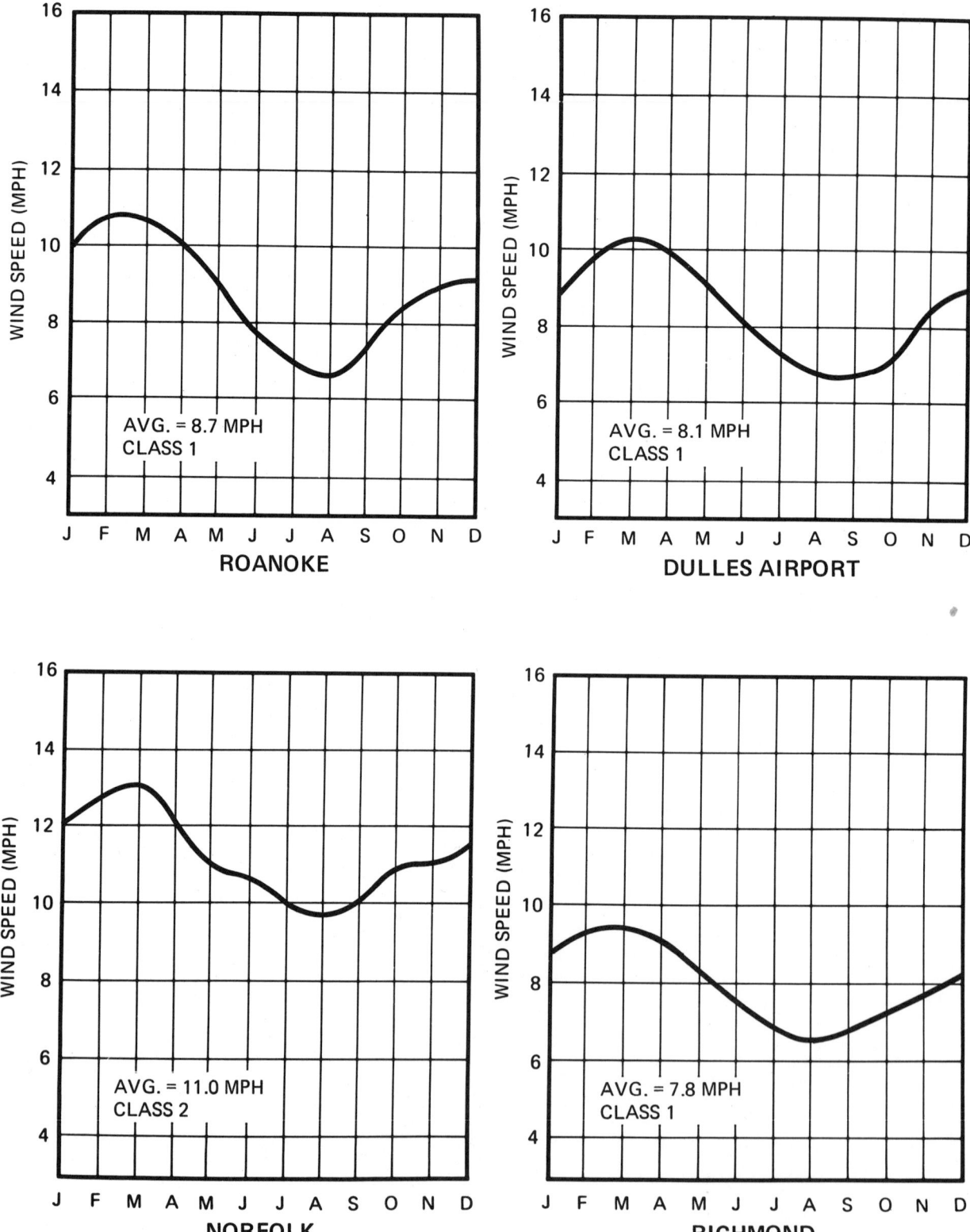

Fig. 43 Monthly average wind speeds in Virginia.

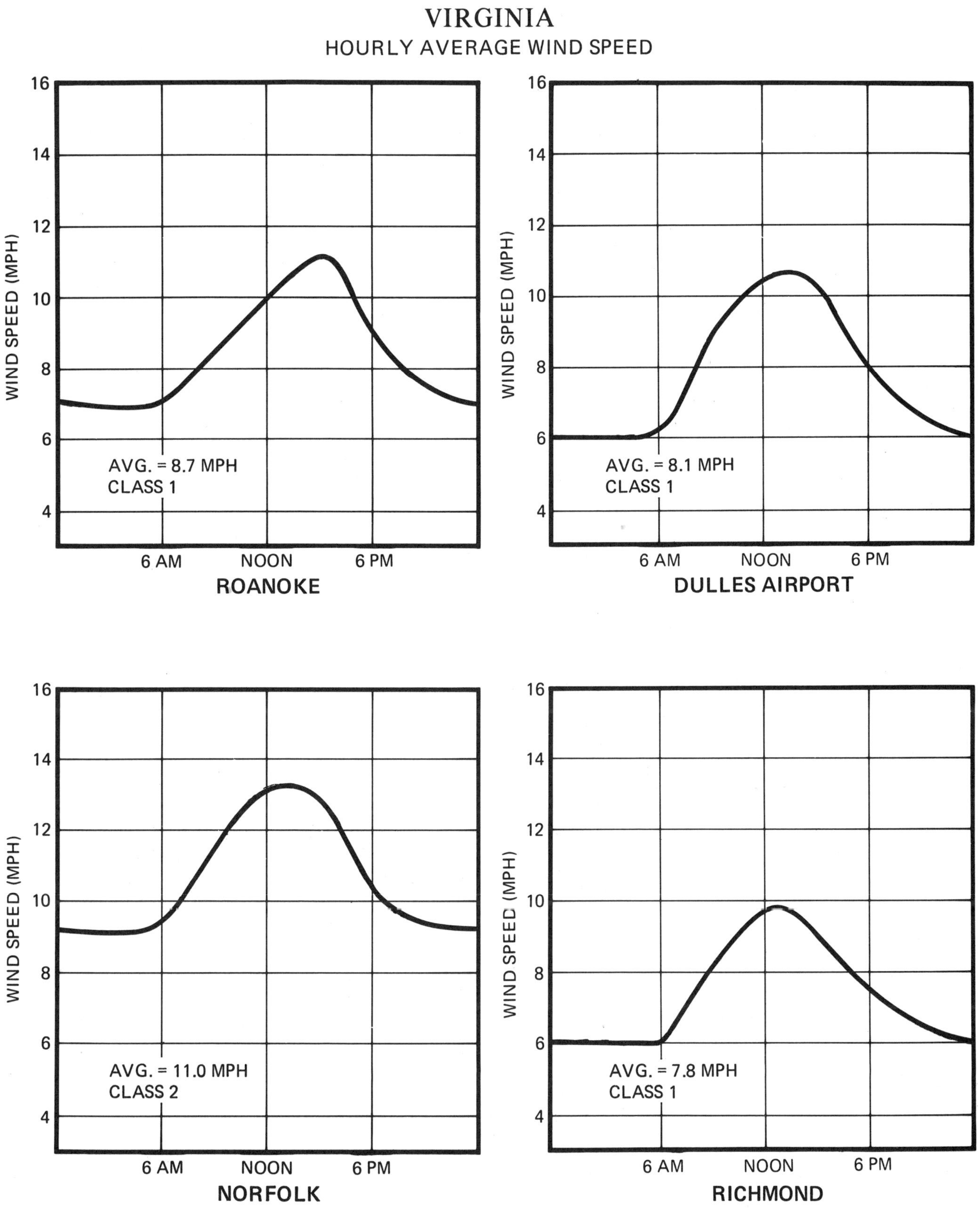
VIRGINIA
HOURLY AVERAGE WIND SPEED
WIND SPEED (MPH)
16
14
12
10
8
6
4
6 AM
NOON
6 PM
AVG. = 8.7 MPH
CLASS 1
ROANOKE
AVG. = 8.1 MPH
CLASS 1
DULLES AIRPORT
AVG. = 11.0 MPH
CLASS 2
NORFOLK
AVG. = 7.8 MPH
CLASS 1
RICHMOND

Fig. 44 Hourly average wind speeds in Virginia.

NORTH CAROLINA

YEARLY AVERAGE WIND SPEEDS

The dampening effects of Dixie on average wind speeds are clearly evident from the map of North Carolina in Fig. 45. For all that, winds are strong on the heights of the Appalachian Mountains and moderate at exposed points on the Atlantic Coast.

The highest surviving peaks of the eroding Appalachian Mountains—several of which exceed 6000 feet—are in extreme western North Carolina. Wind speeds average a blustery Class 5 to Class 6 (13.4 to 15.7 mph) atop these peaks, and Class 2 to 4 over the lesser ridges. Winds are much lighter in the mountain valleys and on the lower slopes. Within a few miles of the Atlantic shores and over Hatteras Island, winds average Class 2 to Class 4; the Class 4 winds are limited to the eastward facing parts of this island.

Apart from the mountaintops and ocean shores, yearly average wind speeds never exceed Class 1, reflecting the calm of this Southern state, sheltered from blustery northern storms.

SEASONAL AVERAGE WIND SPEEDS

Average wind speeds change with the seasons, being strongest in winter and lightest in summer, as shown by Fig. 46. Speeds during the transitional seasons of spring and autumn are shown in Fig. 47.

Winter winds rate Class 7—the highest class—atop most of the Appalachians. Even the lower ridges average Class 5, and some of the rolling foothills adjacent to the mountains rate Class 2. To the oceanfront shores of Hatteras Island, winter brings Class 5 winds; to less exposed coastal sites, Class 2 to Class 4 winds. For all of that, the bulk of North Carolina, between mountain and shore, averages the same Class 1 winds experienced during the rest of the year.

In summer, winds scarcely reach Class 2 even atop the highest mountains and most exposed shores. In spring and autumn, winds fall between the extremes of winter and summer, with spring being the windier of the two.

Monthly average wind speeds at Asheville, Hatteras, Wilmington, and Raleigh are shown in Fig. 48. Winds peak in late winter and early spring regardless of location, with March generally the windiest month. Winds are lightest in the month of August. The difference between the windiest and calmest months is 5 mph at Asheville and 3 to 4 mph at the other three locations.

AVERAGE WIND SPEEDS BY DAY AND NIGHT

Wind speeds across the state increase during the morning and are strongest, on the average, in early afternoon; they then decrease through the evening and remain relatively low until dawn. Figure 49 shows this 24-hour pattern at Asheville, Hatteras, Wilmington, and Raleigh. At Hatteras, which is nearly surrounded by water, the day-night difference amounts to less than 2 mph. By contrast, the inland locations experience a difference of 3 to 5 mph between dawn and afternoon.

72 SOUTH AND SOUTHEAST WIND ATLAS

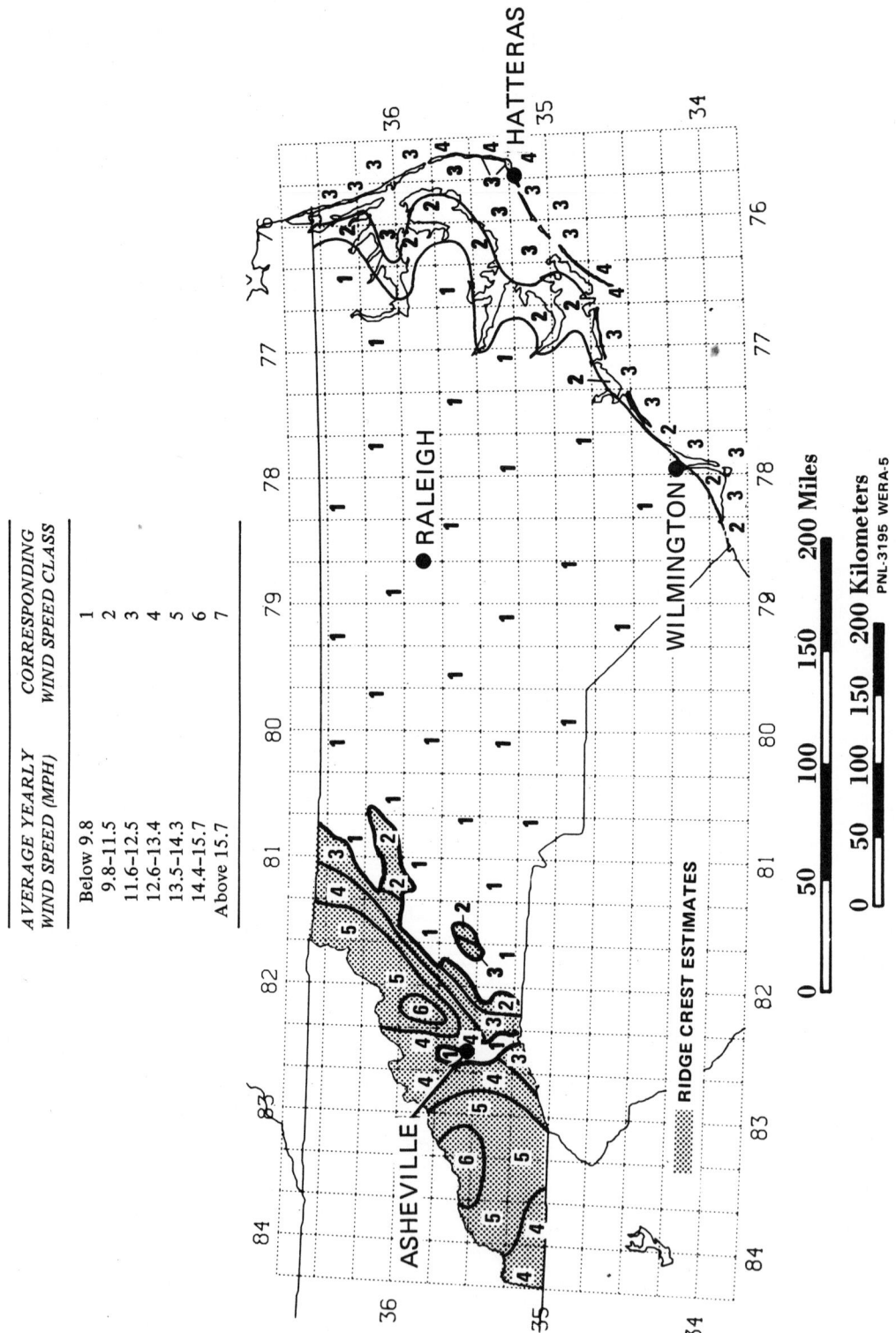

Fig. 45 Yearly average wind speeds in North Carolina.

NORTH CAROLINA 73

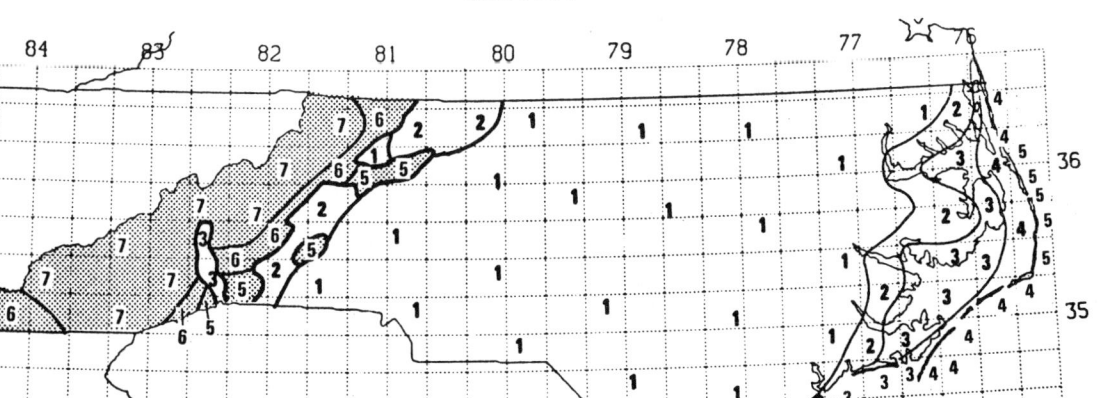

AVERAGE YEARLY WIND SPEED (MPH)	CORRESPONDING WIND SPEED CLASS
Below 9.8	1
9.8–11.5	2
11.6–12.5	3
12.6–13.4	4
13.5–14.3	5
14.4–15.7	6
Above 15.7	7

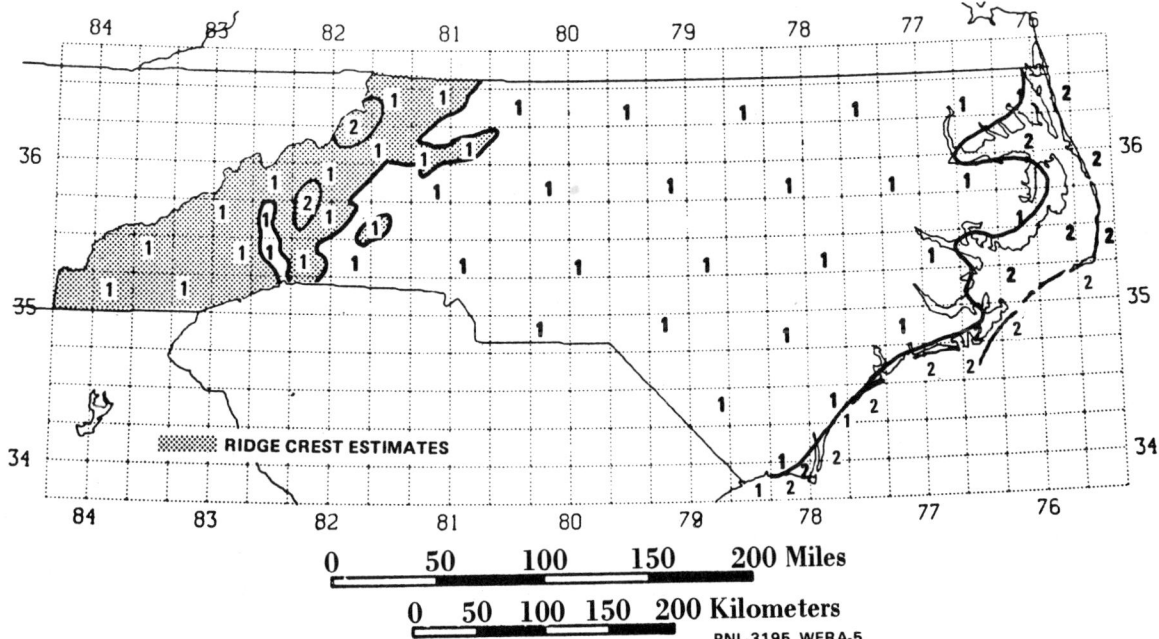

Fig. 46 Seasonal average wind speeds in North Carolina.

74 SOUTH AND SOUTHEAST WIND ATLAS

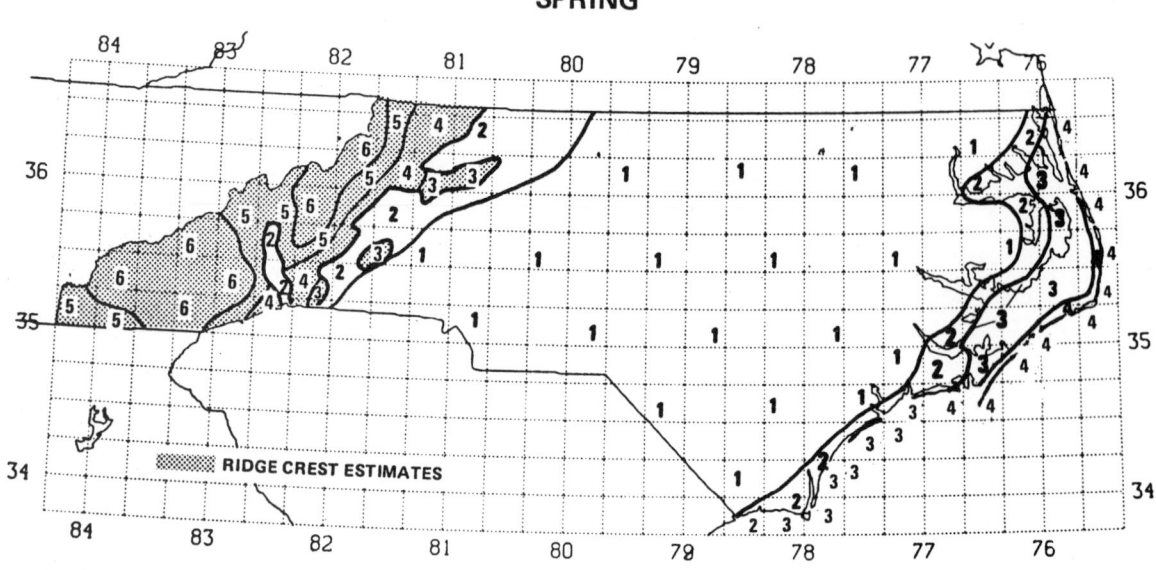

AVERAGE YEARLY WIND SPEED (MPH)	CORRESPONDING WIND SPEED CLASS
Below 9.8	1
9.8–11.5	2
11.6–12.5	3
12.6–13.4	4
13.5–14.3	5
14.4–15.7	6
Above 15.7	7

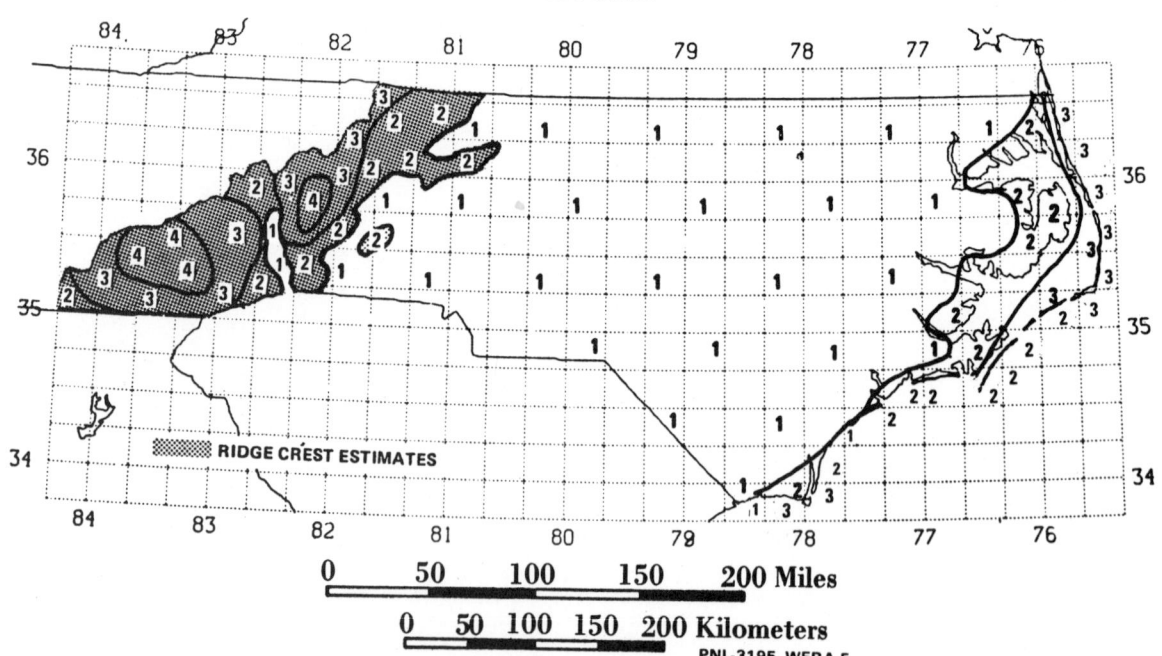

Fig. 47 Seasonal average wind speeds in North Carolina.

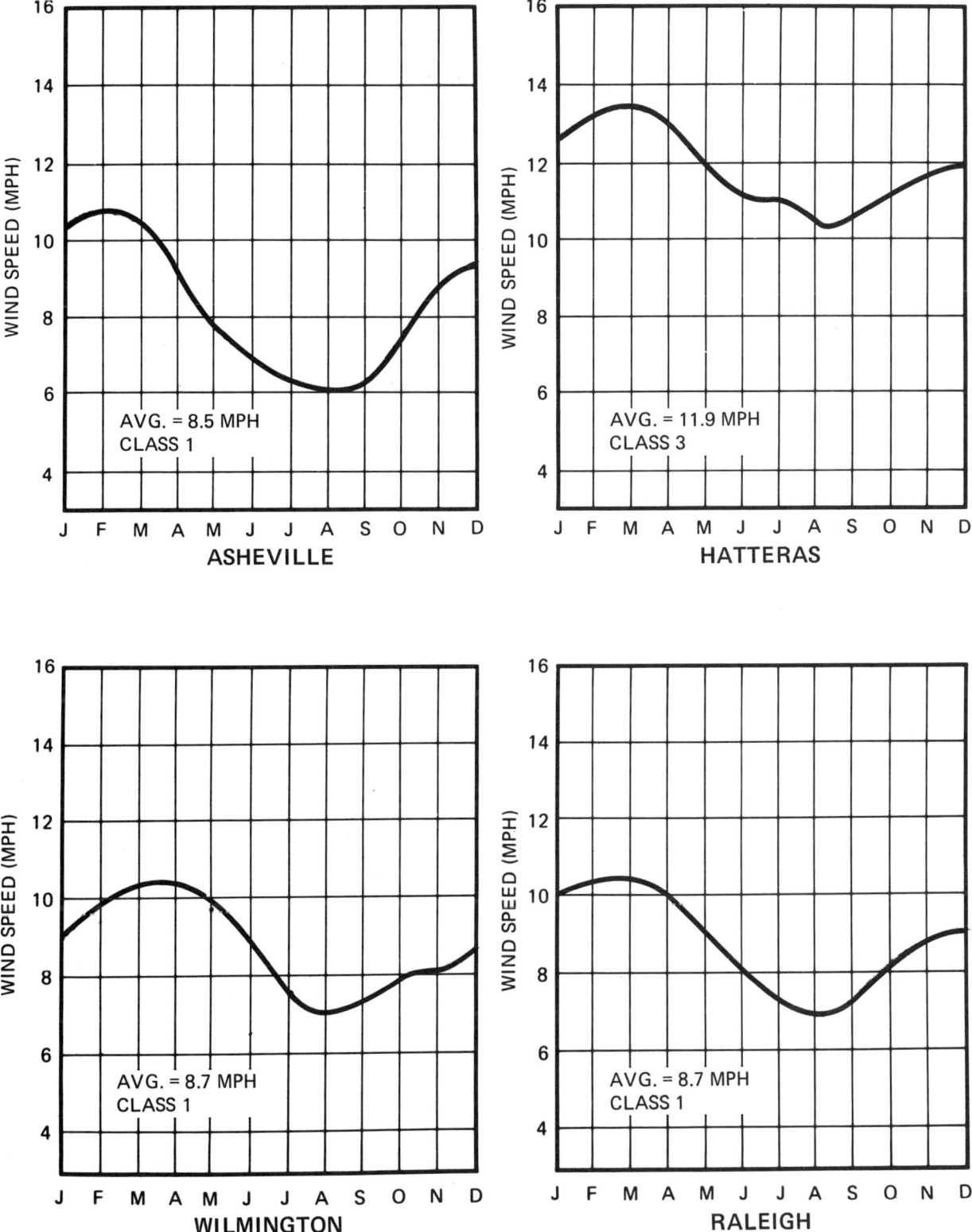

Fig. 48 Monthly average wind speeds in North Carolina.

NORTH CAROLINA
HOURLY AVERAGE WIND SPEED

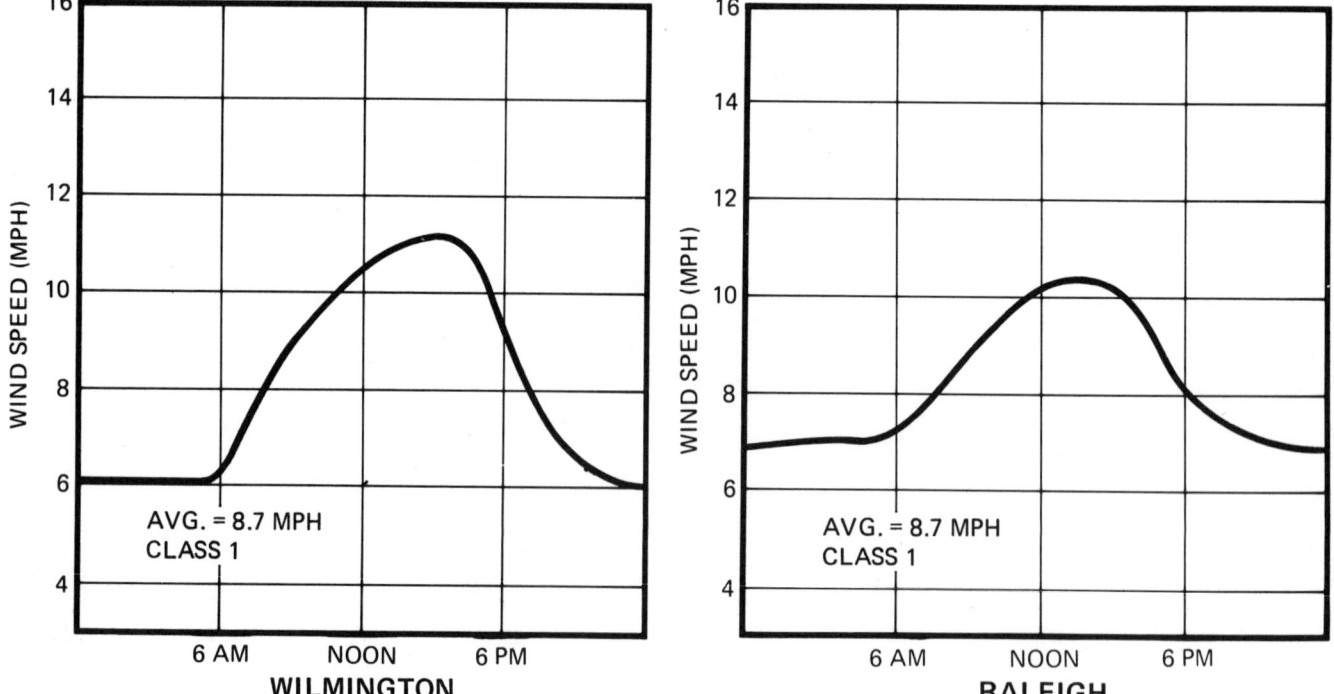

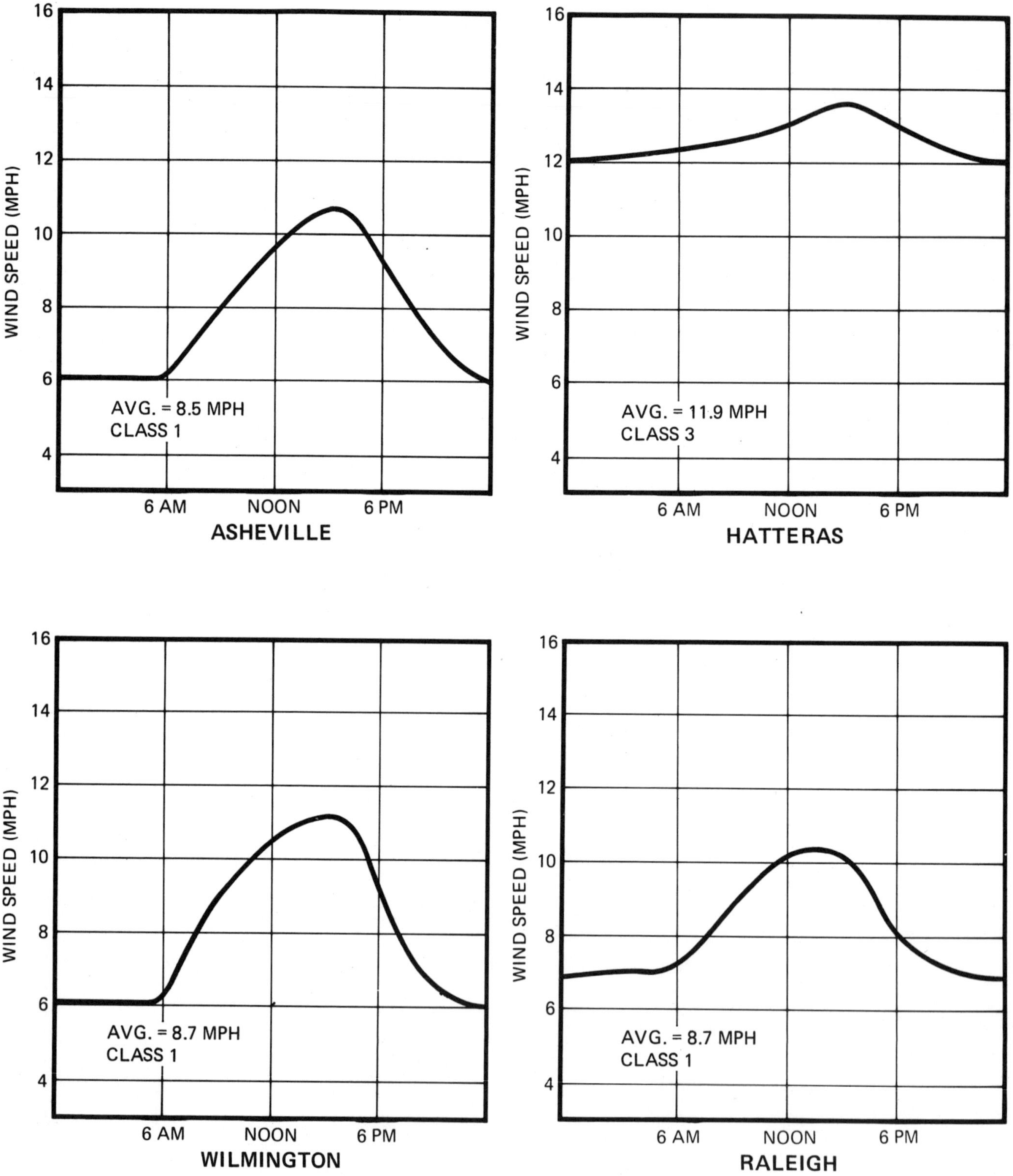

Fig. 49 Hourly average wind speeds in North Carolina.

WIND SPEED AND WIND POWER AT VARIOUS LOCATIONS IN THE EAST CENTRAL REGION

The table that follows shows the yearly average wind speed and the yearly average wind power at each location in the East Central Region where winds are measured frequently and reliably. Not enough measurements have been made at other locations to provide the basis for computing reliable yearly averages. (For a definition of wind power and its relationship to average wind speed, refer to page 3.)

TOWN, CITY, OR PLACE	FACILITY	YEARLY AVERAGE WIND SPEED (MPH AT 33 FT ABOVE GROUND)	YEARLY AVERAGE WIND POWER (WATTS PER SQ. METER)
KENTUCKY			
Bowling Green	Bowling Green City-County Airport	6.9	60
Corbin	Corbin Civil Aeronautics Adm.	5.2	29
Covington	Greater Cincinnati Airport	9.4	88
Fort Campbell	Fort Campbell Air Force Base	6.0	45
Fort Knox	Fort Knox Godman Air Force Base	6.7	61
Lexington	Lexington Blue Grass Field	9.2	76
London	London Municipal Airport	6.0	35
Louisville	Louisville Standiford Field	9.0	75
Paducah	Paducah Barkley Airport	8.1	75
TENNESSEE			
Bristol	Bristol Tri-City Airport	5.8	39
Chattanooga	Chattanooga Lovell Field	6.5	46
Dyersburg	Dyersburg Army Air Field	8.1	68
Memphis	Memphis Naval Air Station	8.1	87
Memphis	Memphis International Airport	9.4	90
Nashville	Nashville Berry Field	9.0	76
Smithville	Smithville Civil Aeronautics Adm.	7.4	52
Smyrna	Stewart Air Force Base	5.2	39
Tullahoma	Tullahoma Northern Airport	4.9	57
WEST VIRGINIA			
Beckley	Beckley-Raleigh Memorial County Airport	9.0	75
Charleston	Charleston-Kanewha Airport	6.3	38
Elkins	Elkins-Randolph County Airport	6.9	54
Huntington	Huntington Chesapeake Airport	3.1	17
Huntington	Huntington Tri-State Airport	6.9	42

TOWN, CITY, OR PLACE	FACILITY	YEARLY AVERAGE WIND SPEED (MPH AT 33 FT) ABOVE GROUND)	YEARLY AVERAGE WIND POWER (WATTS PER SQ. METER)
WEST VIRGINIA (continued)			
Martinsburg	Martinsburg Municipal Airport	6.5	70
Morgantown	Morgantown Municipal Airport	7.2	48
Parkersburg	Parkersburg Weather Bureau Office	6.5	45
Petersburg	Petersburg Weather Bureau Office	5.8	31
Wheeling	Wheeling Ohio County Airport	8.5	80
MARYLAND-DELAWARE			
Aberdeen	Phillips Field	8.1	86
Annapolis	Annapolis Naval Air Facility	7.8	62
Baltimore	Dunkirk Airport	10.8	150
Baltimore	Friendship International Airport	9.4	94
Frederick	Camp Detrick Air Field	6.0	70
Ft. Meade	Tipton Air Force Base	5.4	46
Patuxent River	Patuxent River Naval Air Station	8.5	86
Salisbury	Wicomico County Airport	8.5	84
Washington, D.C.	Andrews Air Force Base	9.0	118
Washington, D.C.	Bolling Field	6.5	56
Dover	Dover Air Force Base	8.7	102
Wilmington	Greater Wilmington/New Castle Airport	10.1	112
VIRGINIA			
Blackstone	Blackstone Civil Aeronautics Adm.	7.8	55
Charlottesville	Charlottesville Albemarle Airport	6.5	35
Chincoteague	Chincoteague Naval Air Station	10.8	126
Danville	Danville Municipal Airport	7.2	47
Davison	Davison Air Force Base	4.7	42
Ft. Eustis	Ft. Eustis Felker Army Air Field	7.2	50
Front Royal	Front Royal Civil Aeronautics Adm.	8.1	89
Gordonsville	Gordonsville Civil Aeronautics Adm.	6.5	49
Hampton	Hampton Langley Air Force Base	9.4	123
Lynchburg	Lynchburg Municipal Airport	7.6	51
Norfolk	Norfolk Naval Air Station	9.4	110
Norfolk	Norfolk Regional Airport	11.0	138

TOWN, CITY, OR PLACE	FACILITY	YEARLY AVERAGE WIND SPEED (MPH AT 33 FT ABOVE GROUND)	YEARLY AVERAGE WIND POWER (WATTS PER SQ. METER)
	VIRGINIA (continued)		
Oceana	Oceana Naval Air Station	7.8	77
Pulaski	Pulaski New River Airport	9.0	87
Quantico	Quantico Marine Corps Air Station	6.3	43
Richmond	Richmond Byrd Field	7.8	53
Roanoke	Roanoke Woodrum Field	8.7	78
Urbanna	Urbanna Aviation Reports	7.8	49
Wallops Island	Wallops Island Weather Bureau Office	11.2	155
Dulles Airport	Dulles Airport	8.1	79
Washington, D.C.	Washington National Airport	9.6	95
	NORTH CAROLINA		
Asheville	Asheville Municipal Airport	8.5	86
Cape Hatteras	Cape Hatteras Weather Bureau Office	11.4	137
Charlotte	Charlotte-Douglas Municipal Airport	7.8	54
Cherry Point	Cherry Point Marine Corps Air Station	7.4	63
Elizabeth City	Elizabeth City Flight Service Station	9.4	81
Fayetteville	Pope Air Force Base	5.4	40
Ft. Bragg	Ft. Bragg Simmons Field	4.9	28
Goldsboro	Seymour-Johnson Air Force Base	6.3	49
Greensboro	Greensboro–High Point Airport	7.8	55
Hatteras	Hatteras Weather Bureau Office	11.9	165
Hickory	Hickory Municipal Airport	5.8	35
Jacksonville	New River Marine Corps Air Field	6.3	46
Lumberton	Lumberton Civil Aeronautics Adm.	6.0	34
New Bern	New Bern Flight Service Station	8.3	56
Raleigh	Raleigh-Durham Airport	8.7	58
Rocky Mount	Rocky Mount Municipal Airport	6.9	48
Wilmington	New Hanover Airport	8.7	75
Winston-Salem	Smith Reynolds Airport	8.1	78

4
Southeast Region

- Mississippi
- Alabama
- Georgia
- South Carolina
- Florida

GENERAL INFORMATION

Although some favorable areas for wind machine operation are available in the Southeastern states, the region as a whole has lower wind speeds than any other in the country. A map of yearly average wind speeds—indicated by wind speed classes—is shown in Fig. 50. Almost the entire region falls in the Class 1 category; that is, wind speeds average less than 9.8 mph. Since an average wind speed of 10 mph is considered the minimum necessary to allow a wind machine to pay for itself, prospects for economical production of wind energy in the Deep South are bleak.

There are some notable exceptions to the prevailing low winds. One promising area is over the ridges of the last gasp of the Appalachian Mountains in northern Alabama, Georgia, and South Carolina. Another is along the coastlines of the Gulf of Mexico and Atlantic Ocean.

The season of strongest average wind speed, as shown in Fig. 51, is spring in South Carolina, eastern Georgia, all but the western panhandle of Florida, and the Gulf coast of Alabama and Mississippi; everywhere else it is winter.

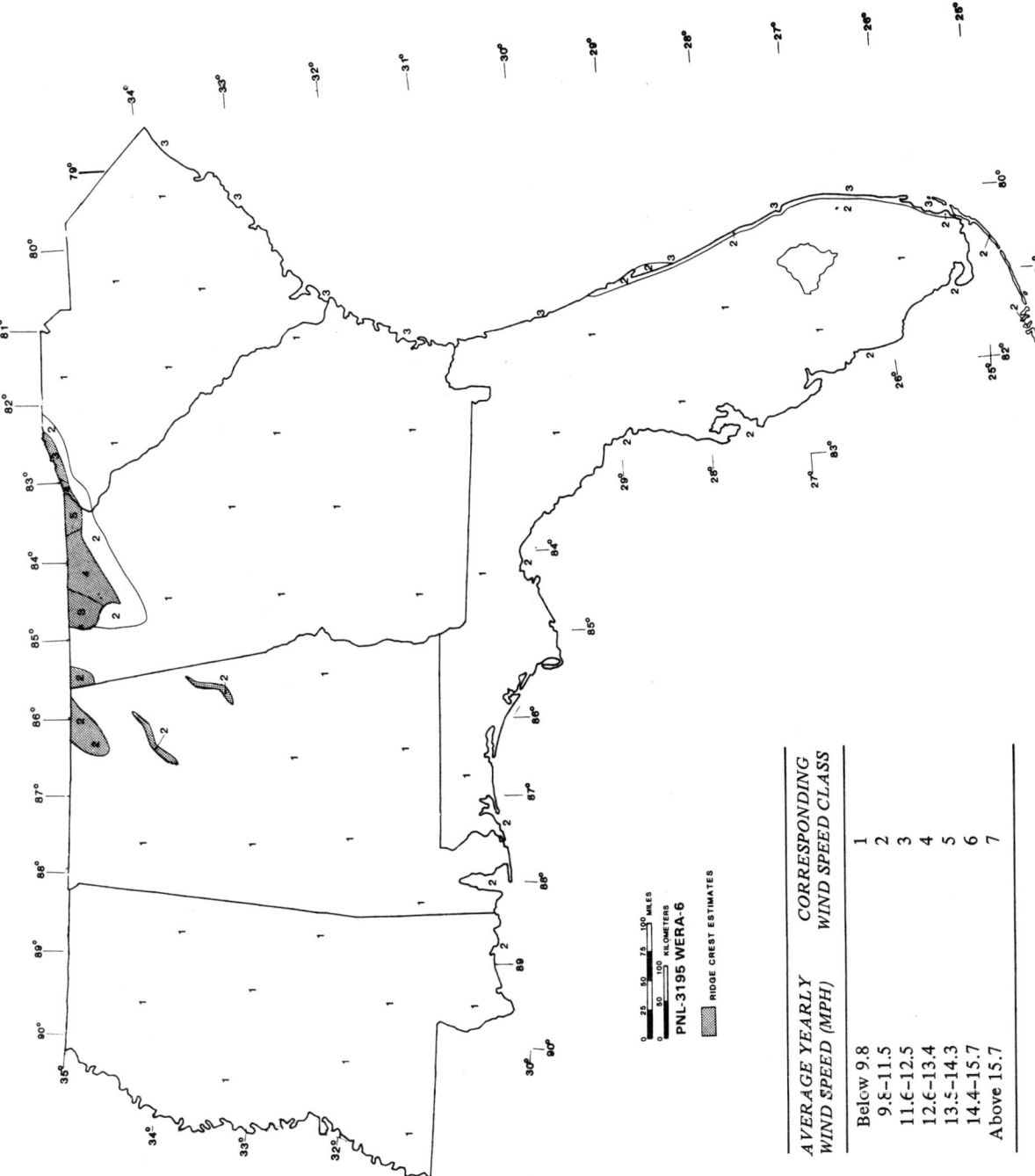

Fig. 50 Yearly average wind speeds in Southeast Region.

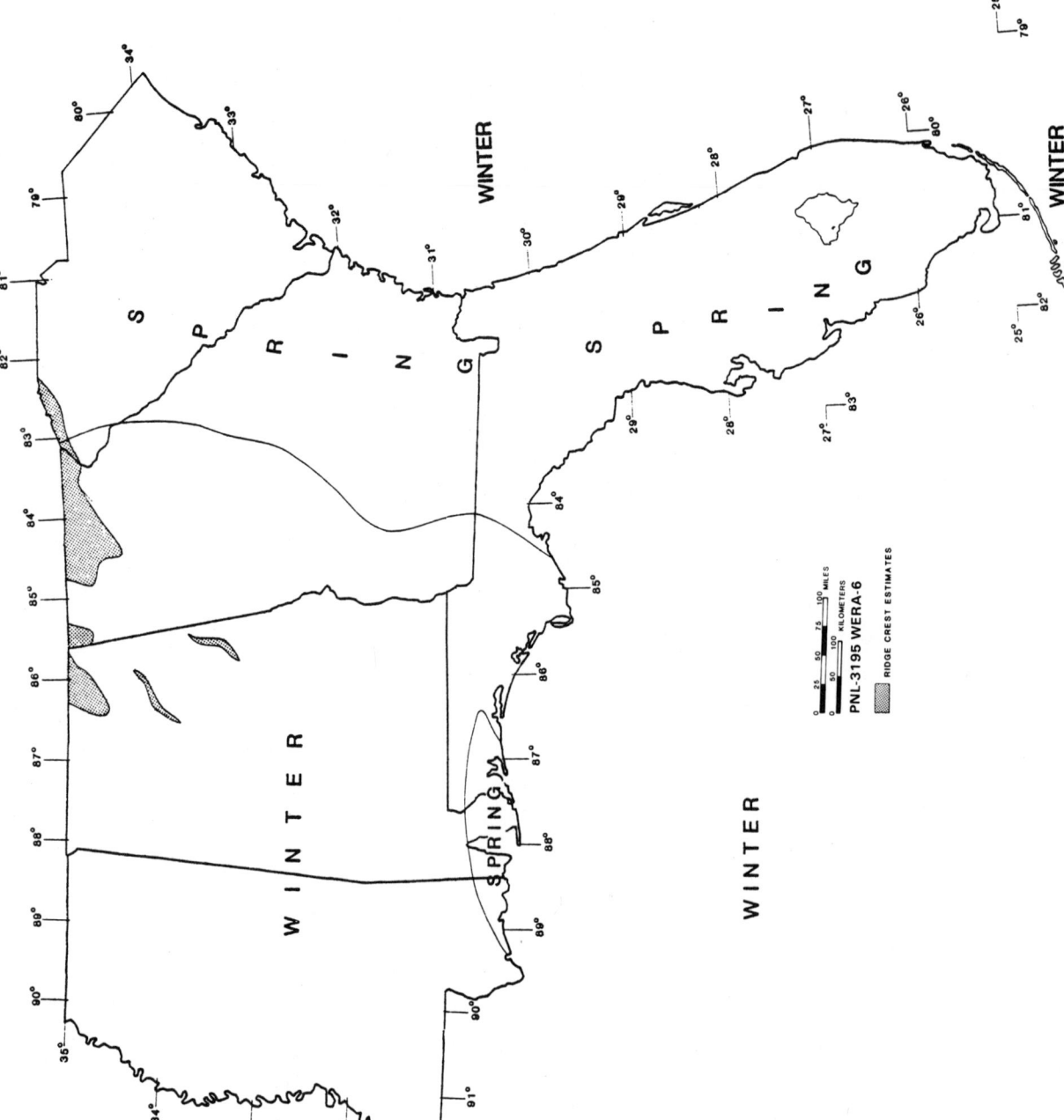

Fig. 51 Seasons of maximum wind speeds in Southeast Region.

MISSISSIPPI

YEARLY AVERAGE WIND SPEEDS

Except along the immediate coast of the Gulf of Mexico, wind speeds over Mississippi average Class 1 (less than 9.8 mph). In fact, Mississippi is the least windy state in the country.

Yearly average wind speeds are shown in Fig. 52. The low wind speeds are due to the state's low latitude, which places it south of customary storm tracks; its lack of significant hills or mountains; and its many forests, which reduce wind speed near the ground, even in large clearings. The only region where winds average as high as Class 2 is along the immediate coast of the Gulf of Mexico, although Class 5 winds are found well offshore.

SEASONAL AVERAGE WIND SPEEDS

Wind speeds in Mississippi change only slightly with the seasons, as shown in Fig. 53, for winter and summer, and Fig. 54, for spring and autumn. Winter—when Class 2 winds blow in the northern part of the state—is the "windiest" season inland. Class 1 winds continue to prevail in the south except for a narrow coastal strip, where Class 2 speeds are also the rule. The arrival of spring pushes the Class 2 winds to the northernmost edge of Mississippi; Class 2 winds continue to blow along the coast.

In both summer and autumn, average winds do not exceed Class 1 anywhere in the state. Moderate or strong winds during thunderstorms usually blow only briefly. Tropical storms bring sustained winds but are much too infrequent to provide significant wind power.

Monthly average wind speeds at four Mississippi locations—Jackson, Biloxi, Columbus, and Meridian—are shown in Fig. 55. Winds are Class 1 at each location. At the Biloxi station, the city to its south reduces the prevailing south to north winds. Winds are probably Class 2 at points near Biloxi that are directly exposed to the Gulf of Mexico. Winds are particularly light at Columbus and Meridian.

The windiest month is March or April at all four locations, and the calmest month is August. The difference between March and August wind speeds is 3 to 4 mph.

WIND SPEEDS BY DAY AND NIGHT

In Mississippi, winds are strongest as a rule during early afternoon and lightest at night. The change of wind speed by hour of the day and night is shown in Fig. 56 for Jackson, Biloxi, Columbus, and Meridian. Afternoon winds at all four locations average about twice as strong as the winds at sunrise. Since the power of the wind to move the blades of a wind machine increases as the cube of its speed, profitable operation of a wind machine is a much better bet during daylight hours than at night.

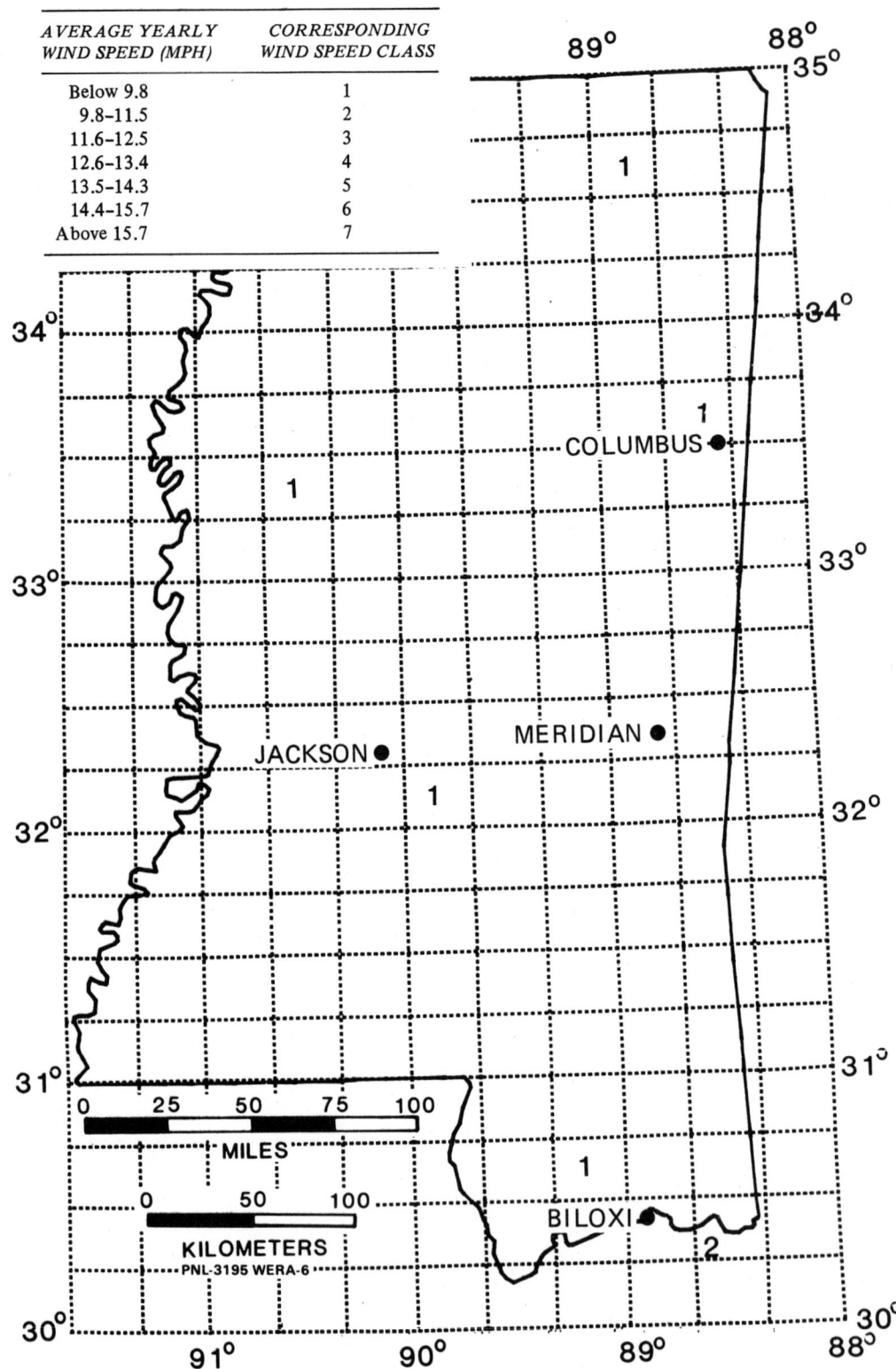

Fig. 52 Yearly average wind speeds in Mississippi.

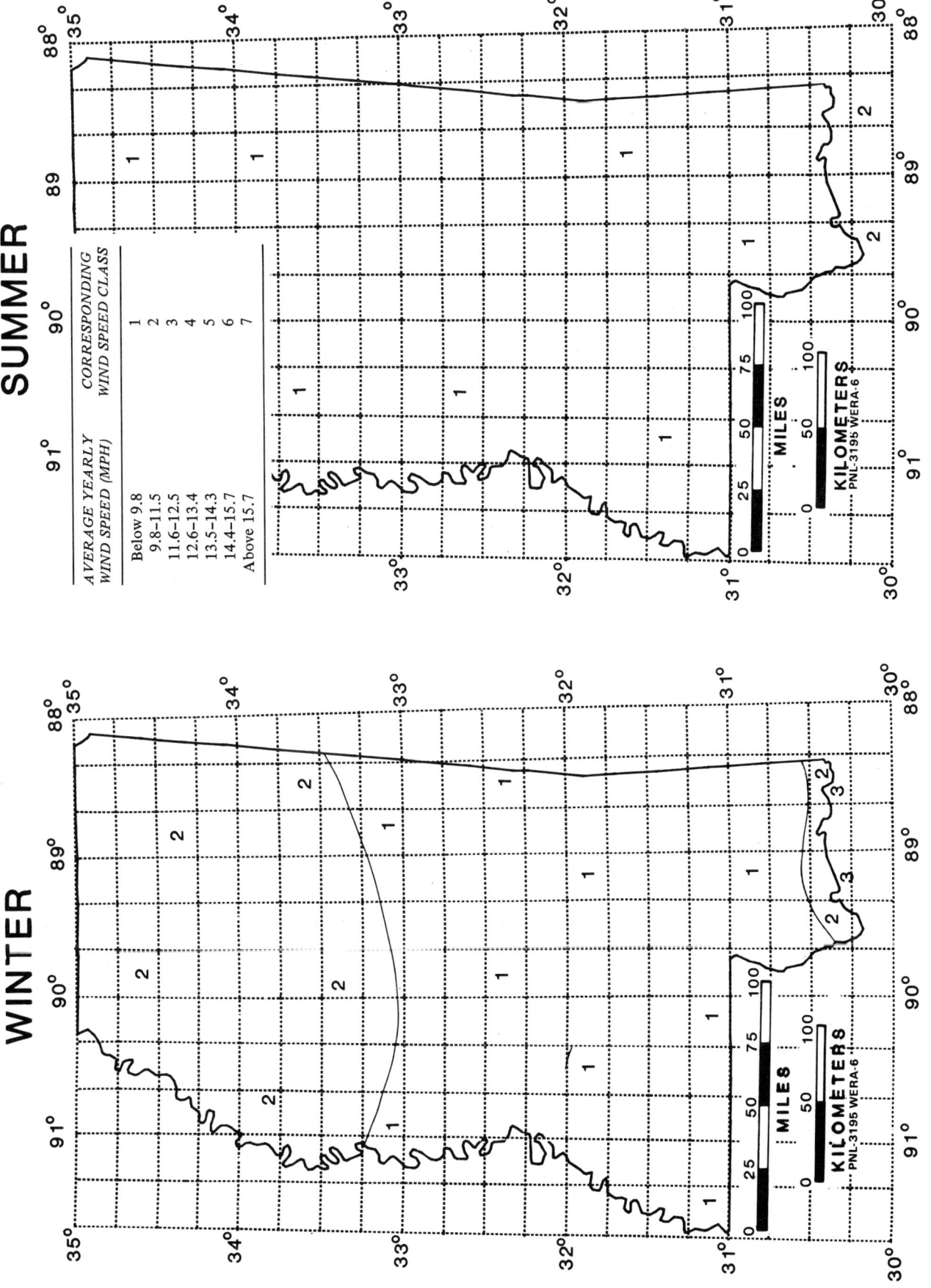

Fig. 53 Seasonal average wind speeds in Mississippi.

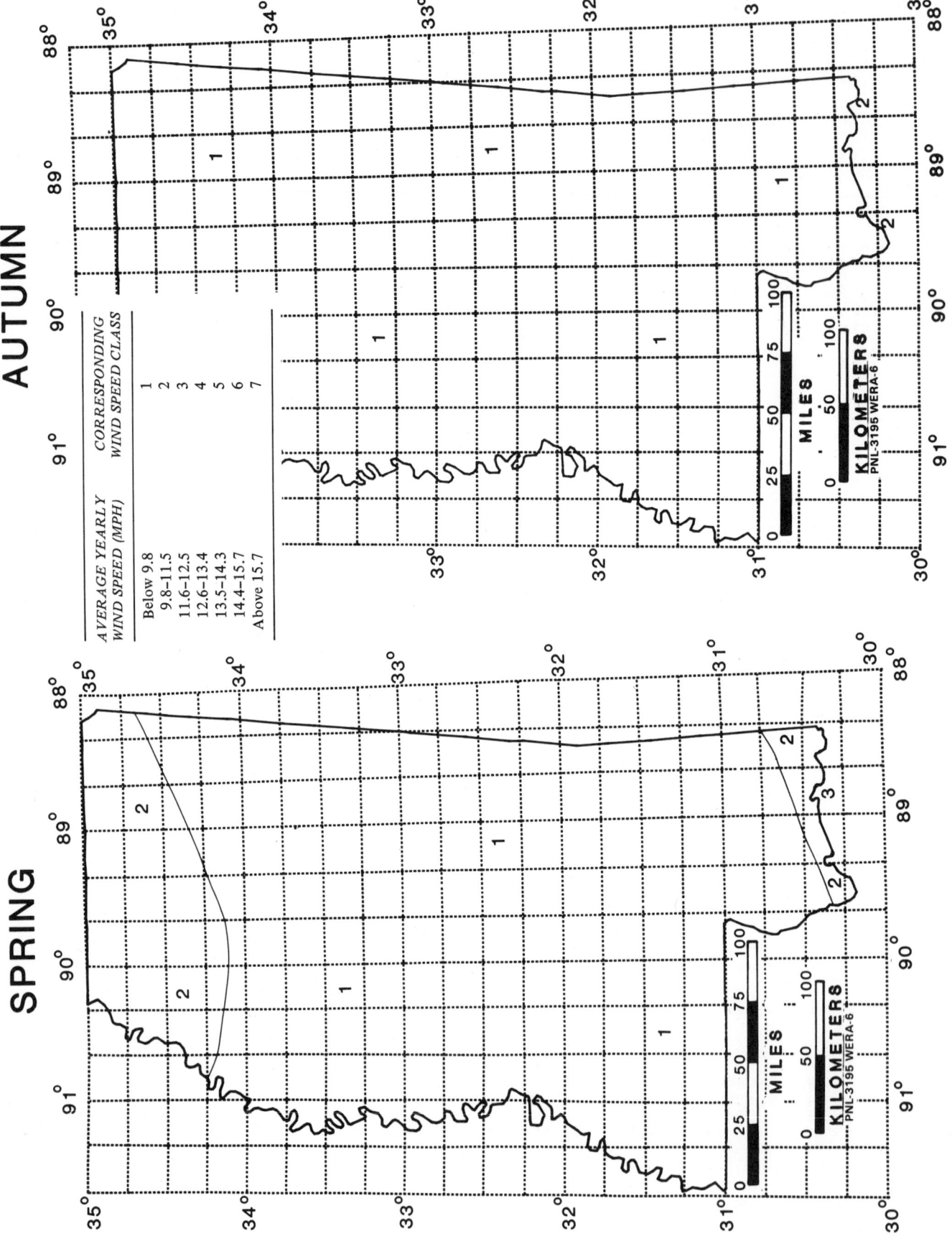

Fig. 54 Seasonal average wind speeds in Mississippi.

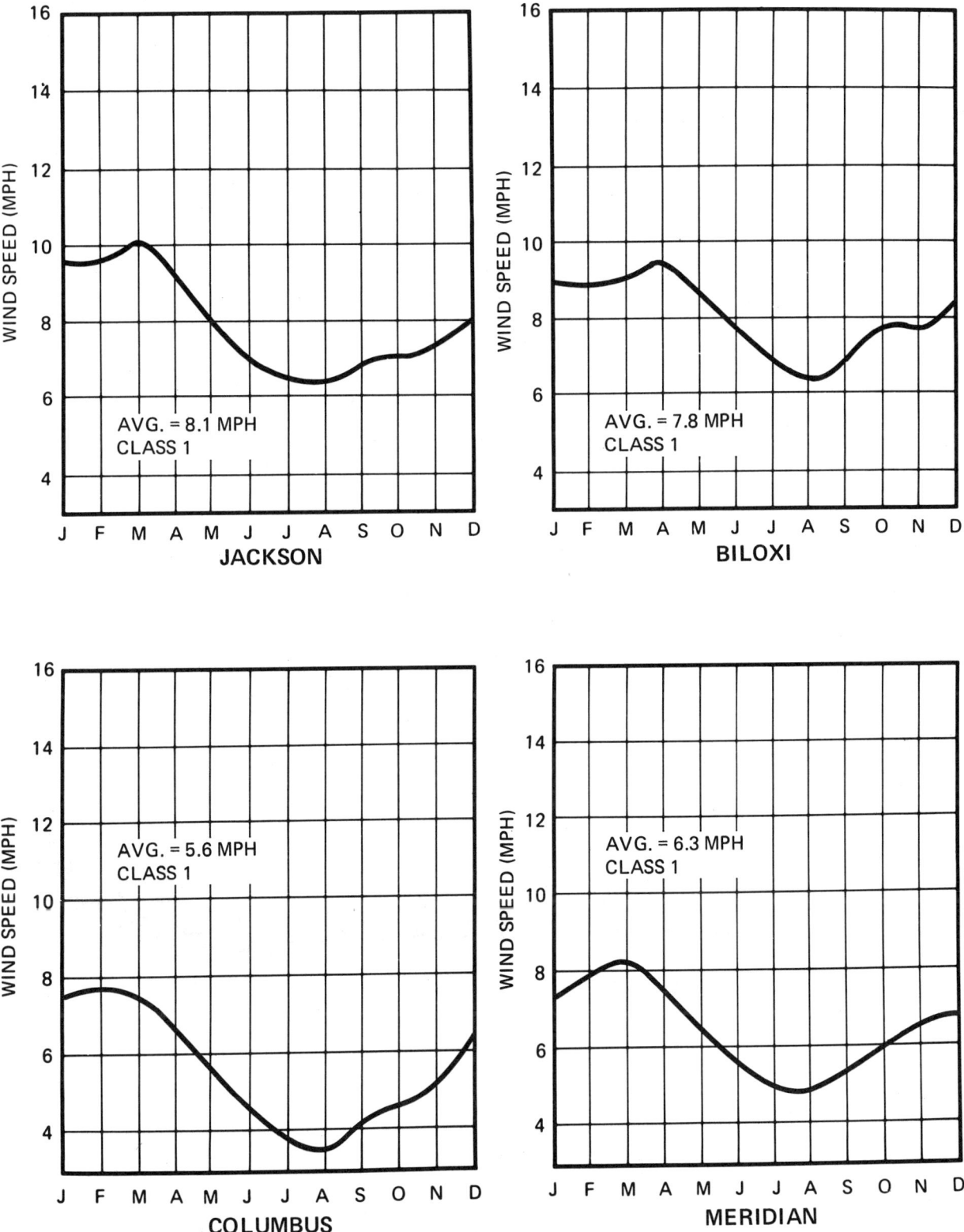

Fig. 55 Monthly average wind speeds in Mississippi.

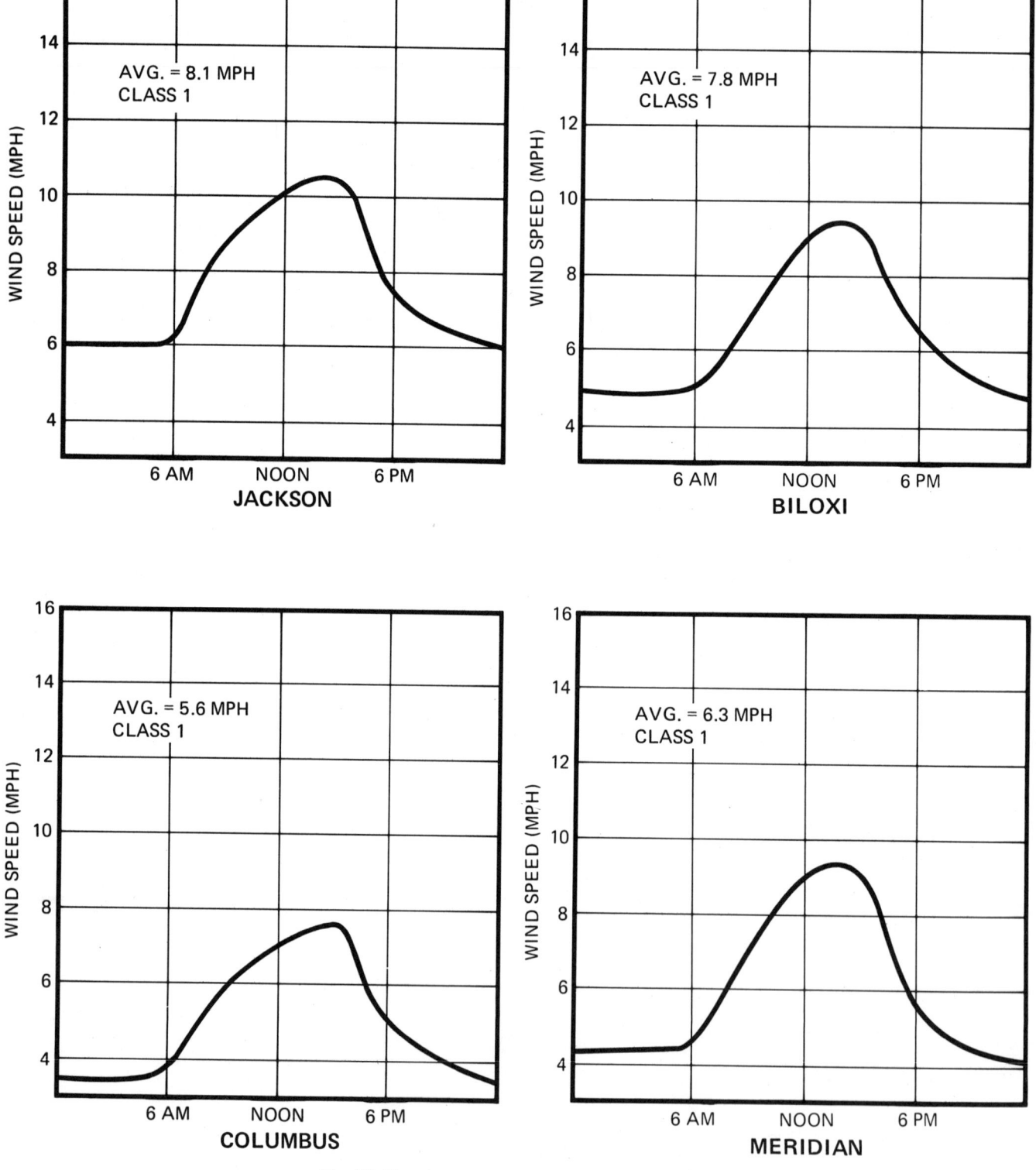

Fig. 56 Hourly average wind speeds in Mississippi.

ALABAMA

YEARLY AVERAGE WIND SPEED

Alabama, in the heart of Dixie, shares the low average wind speeds found in the rest of the south. The state is too far south to benefit from the winds attending the large-scale storm systems that regularly cross the northern and central parts of the country. Only in winter and early spring do occasional storms occur.

Yearly average wind speeds by wind speed class are shown in Fig. 57. All of Alabama experiences Class 1 winds (less than 9.8 mph) except for the coast of the Gulf of Mexico and the ridge crests of the dwindling Appalachian Mountains (shaded areas of Fig. 57), which push into the northeast corner of the state but die out entirely near the center. Winds on these crests are Class 2. Lower mountain slopes and mountain valleys are sheltered and experience only Class 1 winds.

SEASONAL AVERAGE WIND SPEEDS

Average wind speeds during winter and summer are shown in Fig. 58, and those during spring and autumn in Fig. 59. Winter and spring are the windiest seasons in Alabama, but not even these seasons can be properly termed windy inasmuch as Class 1 winds continue to prevail over most of the state. Mountaintops and ridge crests enjoy winter winds of Class 3 to Class 4, however, and even the lower elevations near the mountains, as well as the northwest corner of the state and the Mobile Bay area, experience Class 2 winds. The pattern in spring is similar to that in winter, although winds are significantly lighter by May than they are during March, the first month of spring.

Summer is a Class 1 season, the only exception being the immediate Gulf Shore. Autumn wind speeds increase as the season progresses, but the average on the higher mountain ridges is never higher than Class 2.

Monthly average wind speeds at Birmingham, Mobile, Dothan, and Huntsville are shown in Fig. 60. Birmingham is typical of valley locations near mountains. The Mobile graph shows wind speed variation in the Mobile Bay vicinity, but winds are somewhat stronger on the immediate Gulf shore. The remaining locations—Dothan in the south and Huntsville in the north—are typical of inland locations.

At all four locations, March is the windiest month and August the calmest. At Mobile, March is windier than August by about 5 mph; at the other locations, the difference is 4 mph. Since winds usually blow from south to north—especially in the warmer half of the year—wind machines should be located where there are fewest obstructions to the wind south of the wind machine site.

AVERAGE WIND SPEEDS BY DAY AND NIGHT

Average wind speeds over the 24-hour cycle are shown in Fig. 61 for Birmingham, Mobile, Huntsville, and Dothan. At each location, winds reach their minimum during the night, increase during the morning to an afternoon peak, and fall again during the evening. The difference between the afternoon maximum and the nighttime minimum is greatest at Huntsville and Birmingham—5 mph— but is only 3 to 4 mph at Mobile and Dothan. Normally, the difference is greater inland than near the Gulf, on sunny days than on cloudy days, and in early spring than in late summer.

AVERAGE YEARLY WIND SPEED (MPH)	CORRESPONDING WIND SPEED CLASS
Below 9.8	1
9.8–11.5	2
11.6–12.5	3
12.6–13.4	4
13.5–14.3	5
14.4–15.7	6
Above 15.7	7

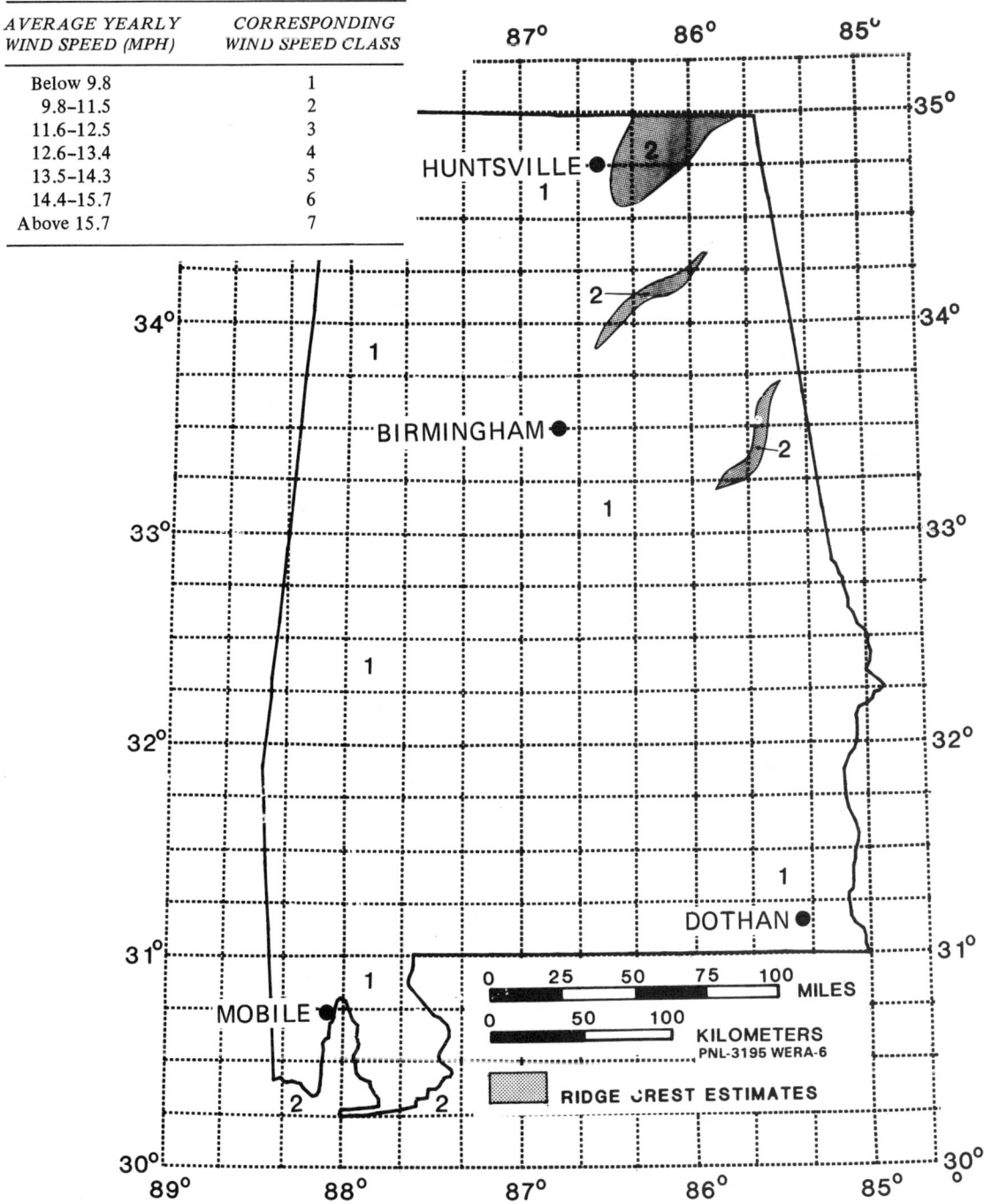

Fig. 57 Yearly average wind speeds in Alabama.

92 SOUTH AND SOUTHEAST WIND ATLAS

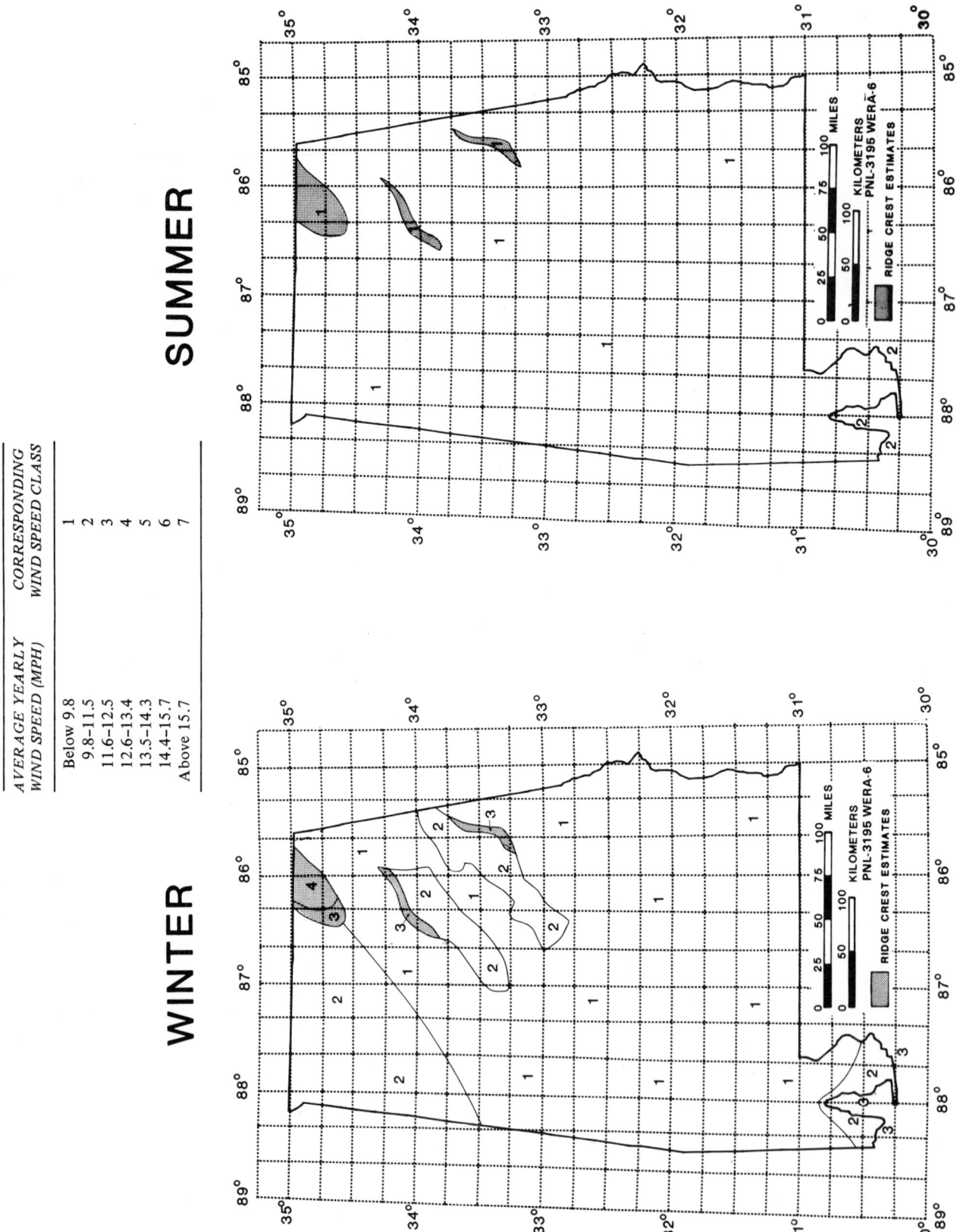

Fig. 58 Seasonal average wind speeds in Alabama.

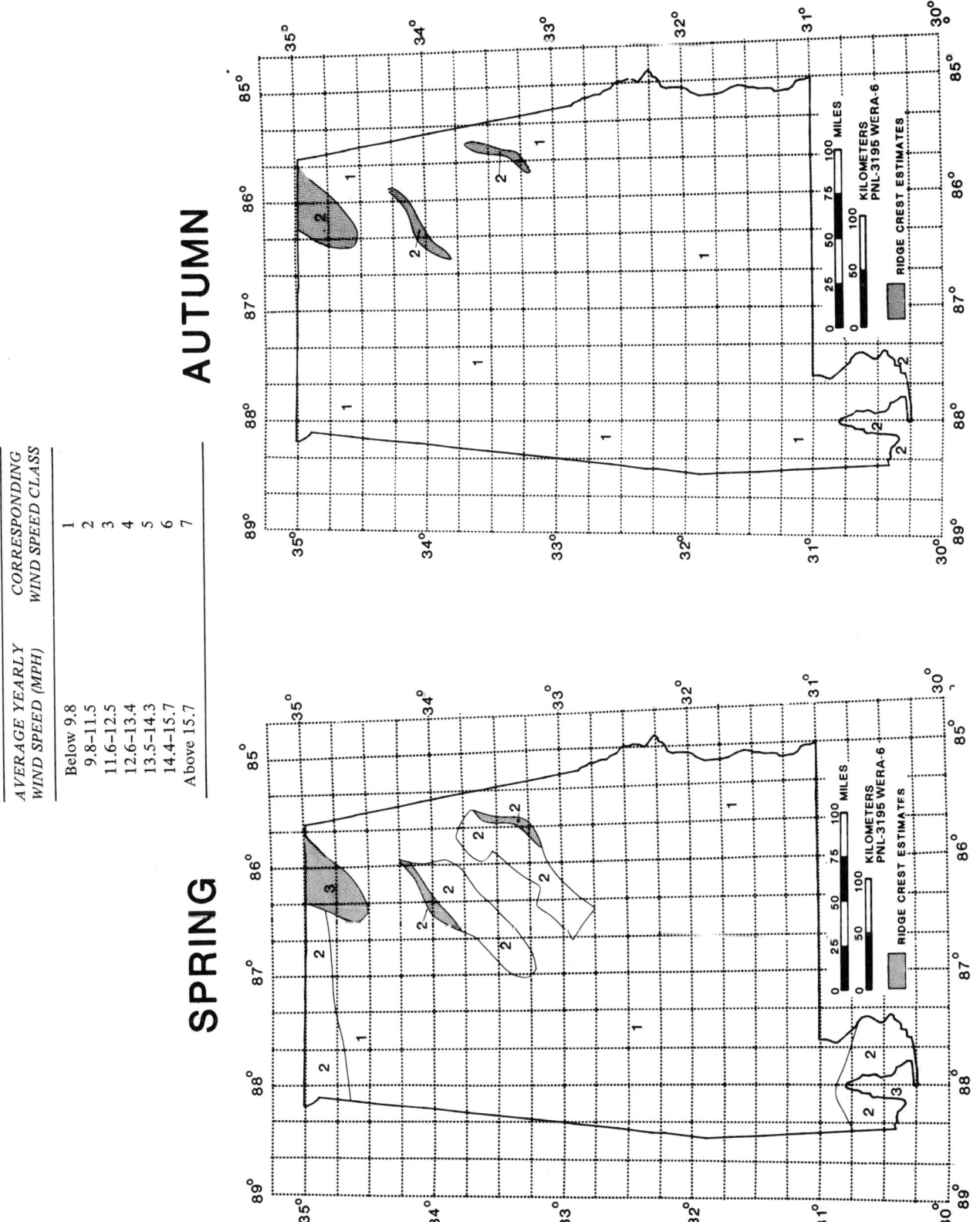

Fig. 59 Seasonal average wind speeds in Alabama.

ALABAMA
MONTHLY AVERAGE WIND SPEED

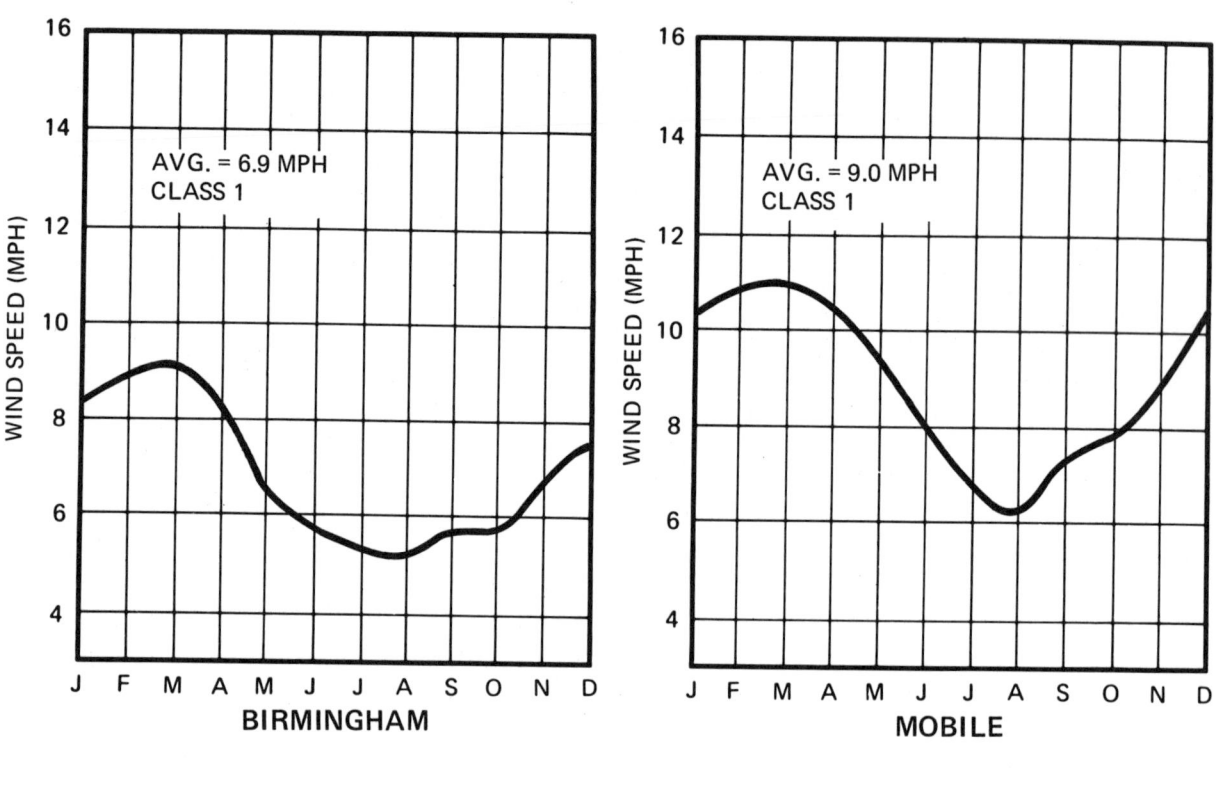
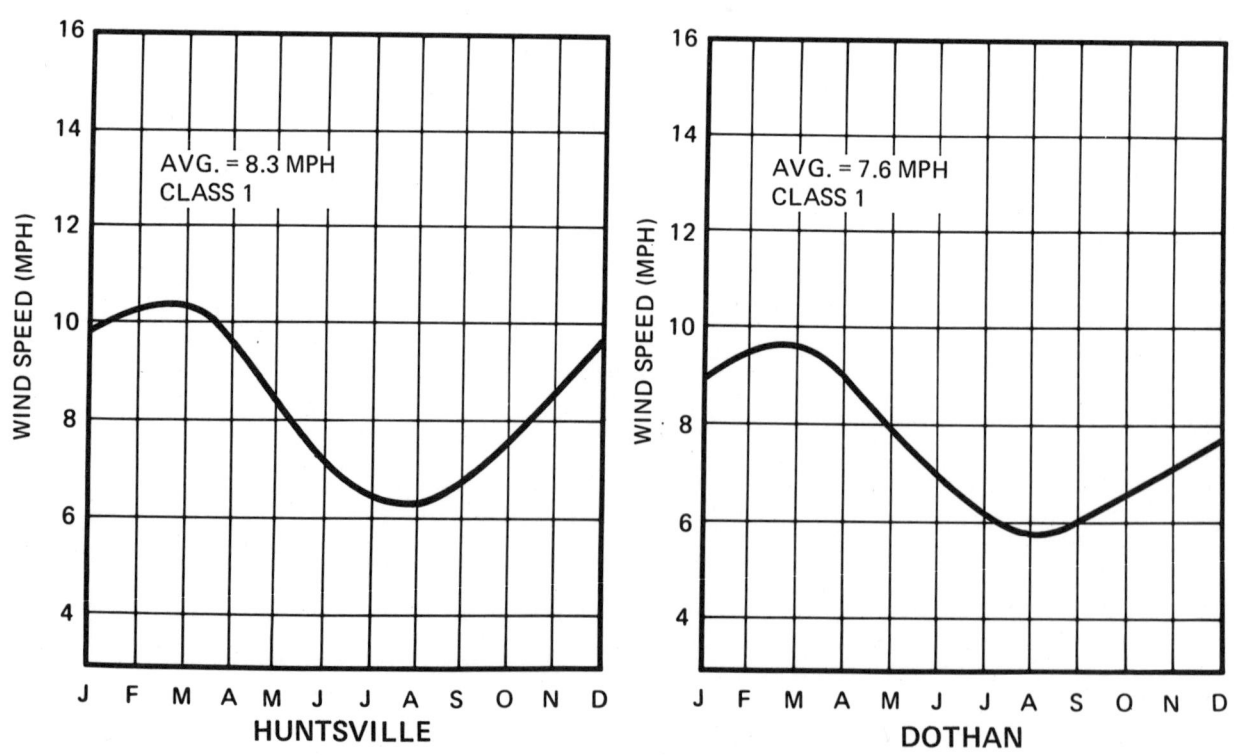

Fig. 60 Monthly average wind speeds in Alabama.

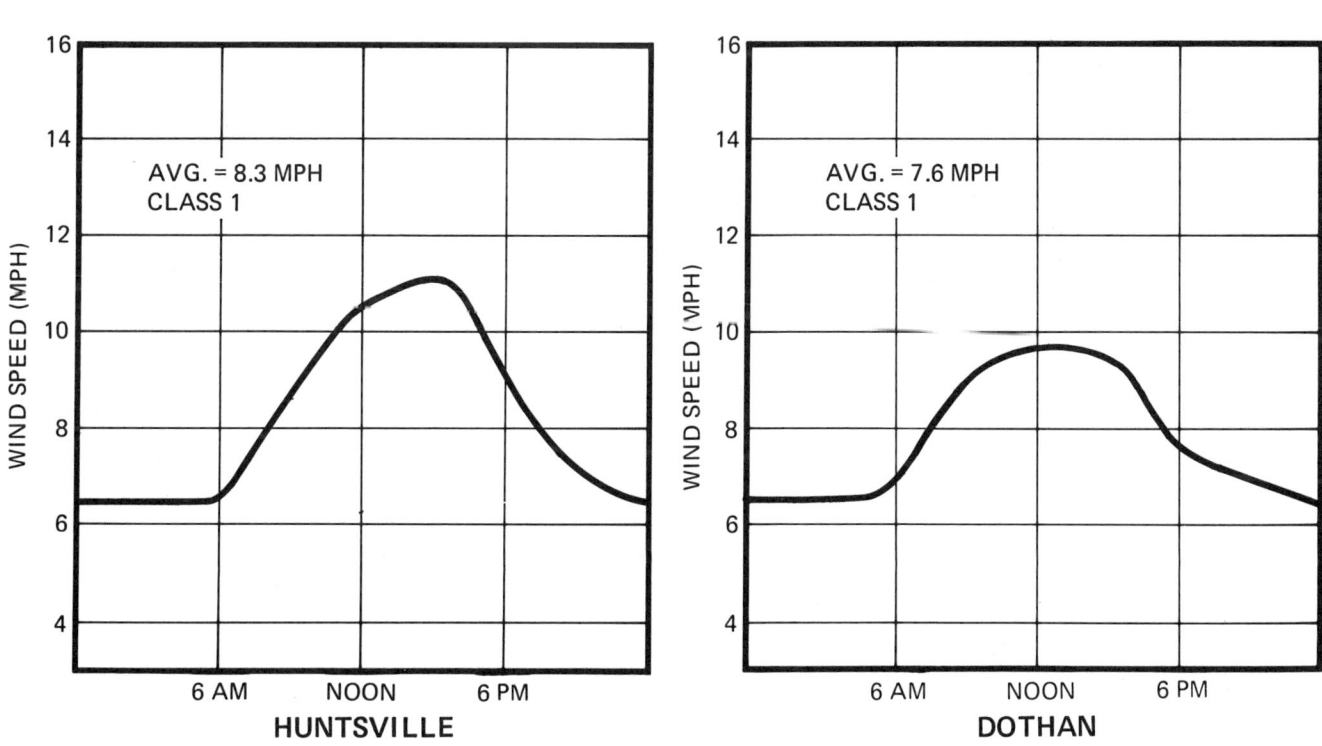

Fig. 61 Hourly average wind speeds in Alabama.

GEORGIA

YEARLY AVERAGE WIND SPEEDS

Wind speeds are too light over 97 percent of Georgia for the profitable operation of a wind machine. Some good wind machine sites can be found in the hilly and mountainous terrain in the north, however, and along the immediate Atlantic coastline.

Figure 62 shows the very limited areas where winds average higher than Class 1 (above 9.8 mph). The Class 2 region represents the foothills of the Blue Ridge Mountains; here winds are as high as Class 2 only on the hilltops. The shaded area indicates the mountainous part of the state, including the lofty Blue Ridge, which terminates some forty miles north of Atlanta. In most of this area—made up of lower mountain slopes and valleys—winds are light. Only on ridge crests do winds blow as hard as Class 3 to 5.

Winds are also as high as Class 3 on the small islands and the shores of the larger bays on the Atlantic coast. Winds decrease rapidly inland, especially along wooded shores.

SEASONAL AVERAGE WIND SPEEDS

Average wind speeds change considerably with the seasons over the high mountain ridges in the extreme north of Georgia. Over the rolling terrain in the rest of the state, there are also seasonal changes, but winds never average more than Class 1 during any season.

Wind speeds for winter and summer are shown in Fig. 63 and for spring and autumn in Fig. 64. The windiest seasons are late winter and early spring. Winter winds average Class 7—the highest class—over the highest parts of the Blue Ridge, and lesser mountain ridges experience winds from Class 3 to Class 6 during both winter and spring. The narrow foothill region offers only Class 2 to Class 3 winds, but these affect a broader area than the stronger winds atop the few mountain ridges.

Winter and spring each provide Class 3 winds on the immediate Atlantic shore and Class 2 winds over a strip that extends a few miles inland. In summer, only the immediate Atlantic shore experiences speeds as high as Class 2; in the rest of the state, Class 1 winds prevail even atop the highest peaks. Autumn winds are nearly as light as those of summer, but a distinct increase occurs in late fall.

Monthly average wind speeds are shown in Fig. 65 for Atlanta, Valdosta, Macon, and Augusta. March is the windiest month at each location, and August is the least windy. The change from month to month is small when compared with that of more northerly locations. The difference between the windiest and calmest months amounts to 4 mph at Atlanta and less than 3 mph at the other three sites.

AVERAGE WIND SPEEDS BY DAY AND NIGHT

The change in average wind speed from day to night is quite large. Winds are ordinarily lightest from midnight to sunrise and strongest during the early afternoon. Changes over the 24-hour cycle are shown in Fig. 66 for Atlanta, Valdosta, Macon, and Augusta. During the speed peak in the afternoon, winds are around 10 mph at all four locations. The nighttime minimum is about 5 mph, except at Atlanta, where it is 7 mph.

At all locations, winds vary more on sunny days than on cloudy ones and more during late spring and summer than in late autumn and winter.

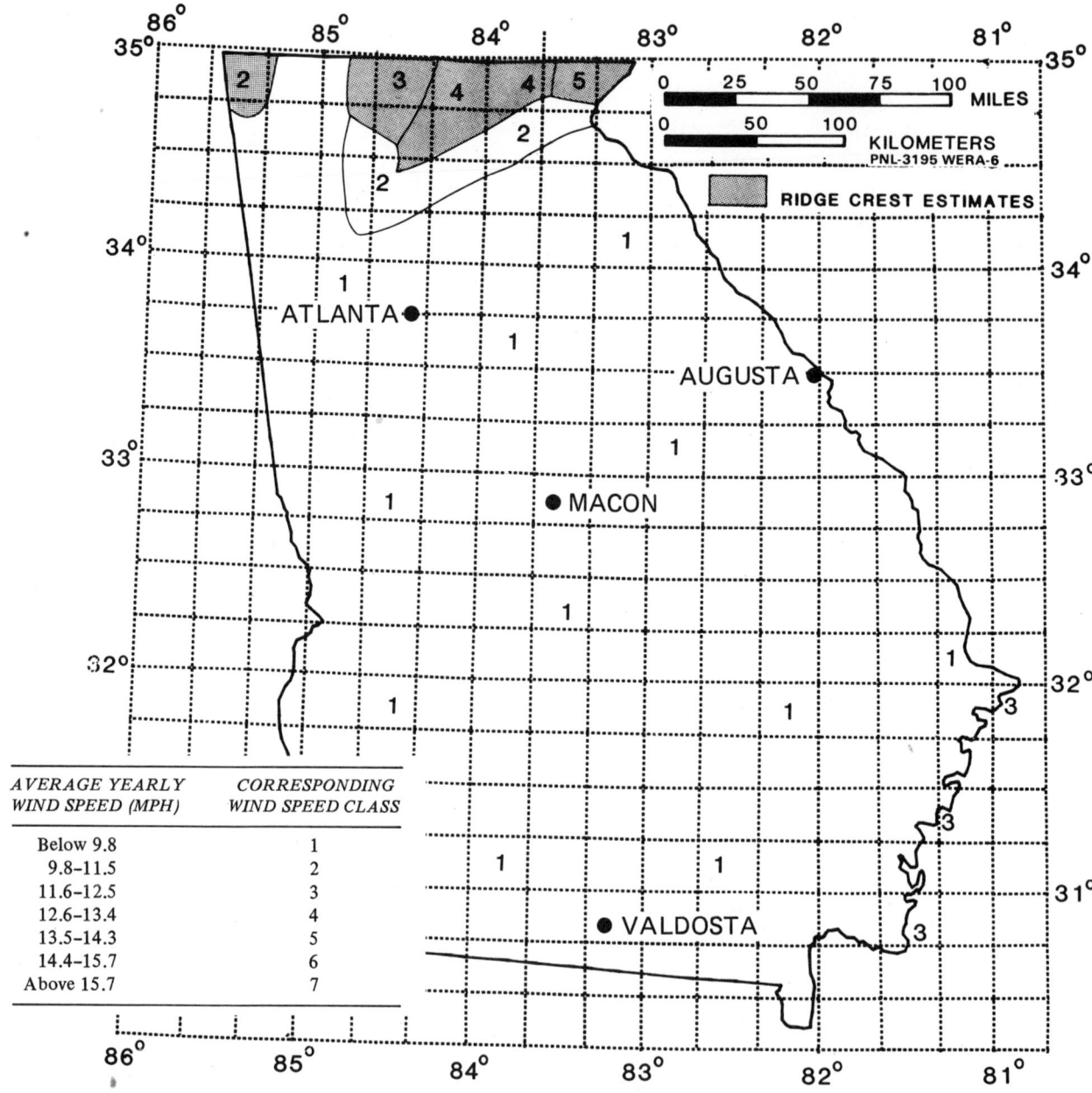

Fig. 62 Yearly average wind speeds in Georgia.

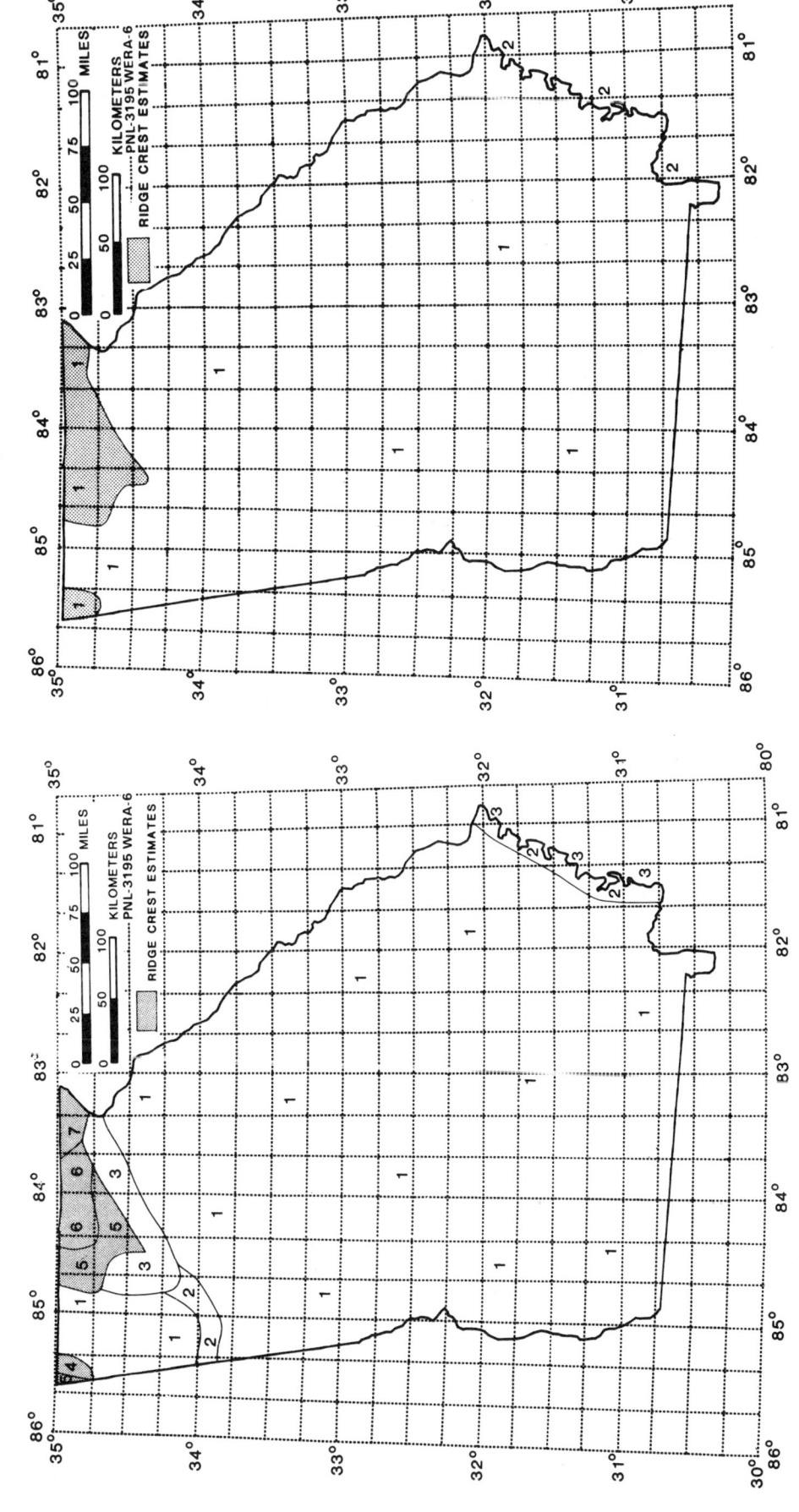

Fig. 63 Seasonal average wind speeds in Georgia.

AVERAGE YEARLY WIND SPEED (MPH)	CORRESPONDING WIND SPEED CLASS
Below 9.8	1
9.8–11.5	2
11.6–12.5	3
12.6–13.4	4
13.5–14.3	5
14.4–15.7	6
Above 15.7	7

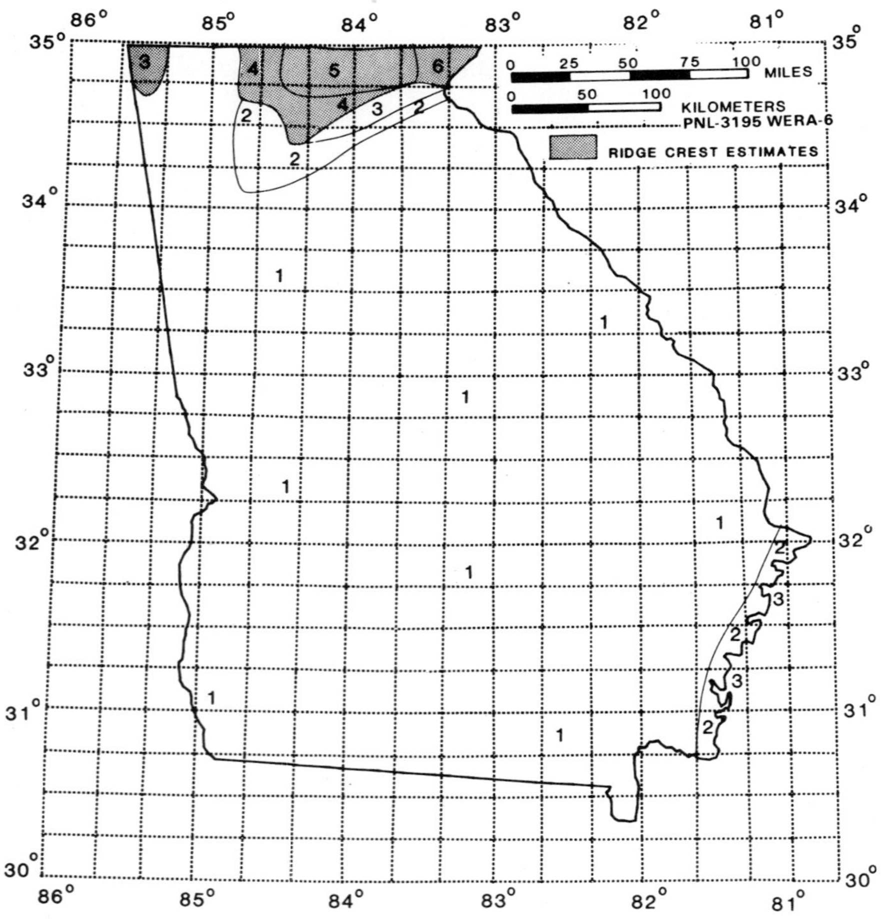

AUTUMN

SPRING

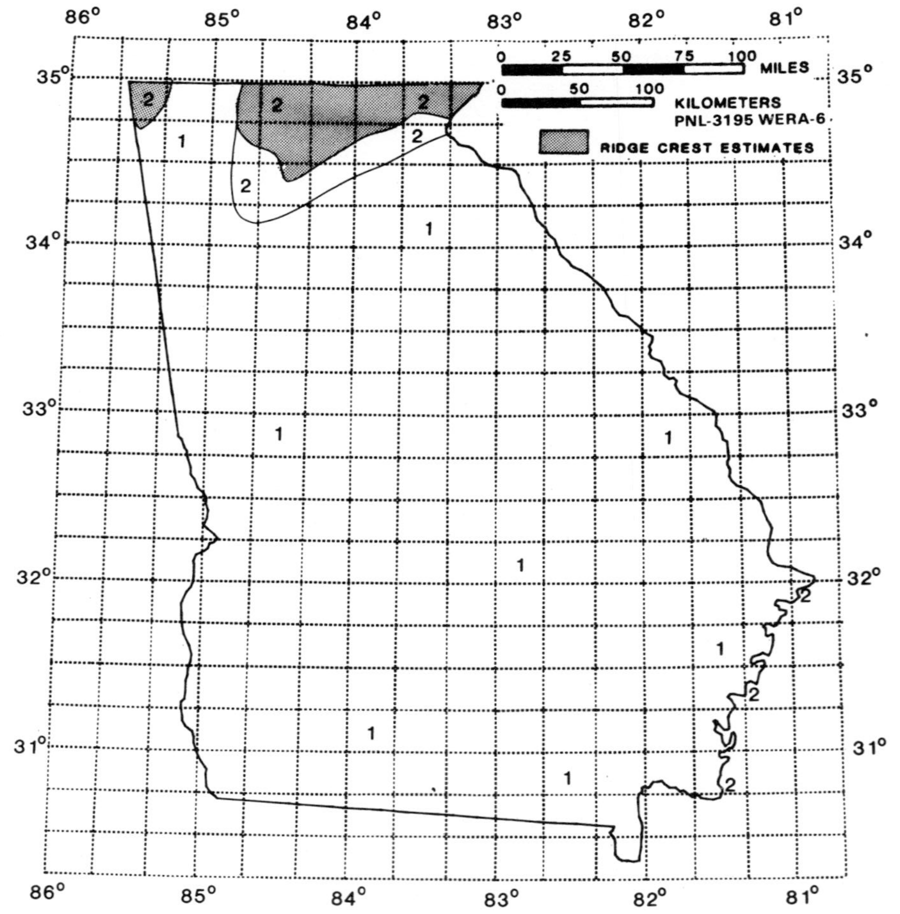

Fig. 64 Seasonal average wind speeds in Georgia.

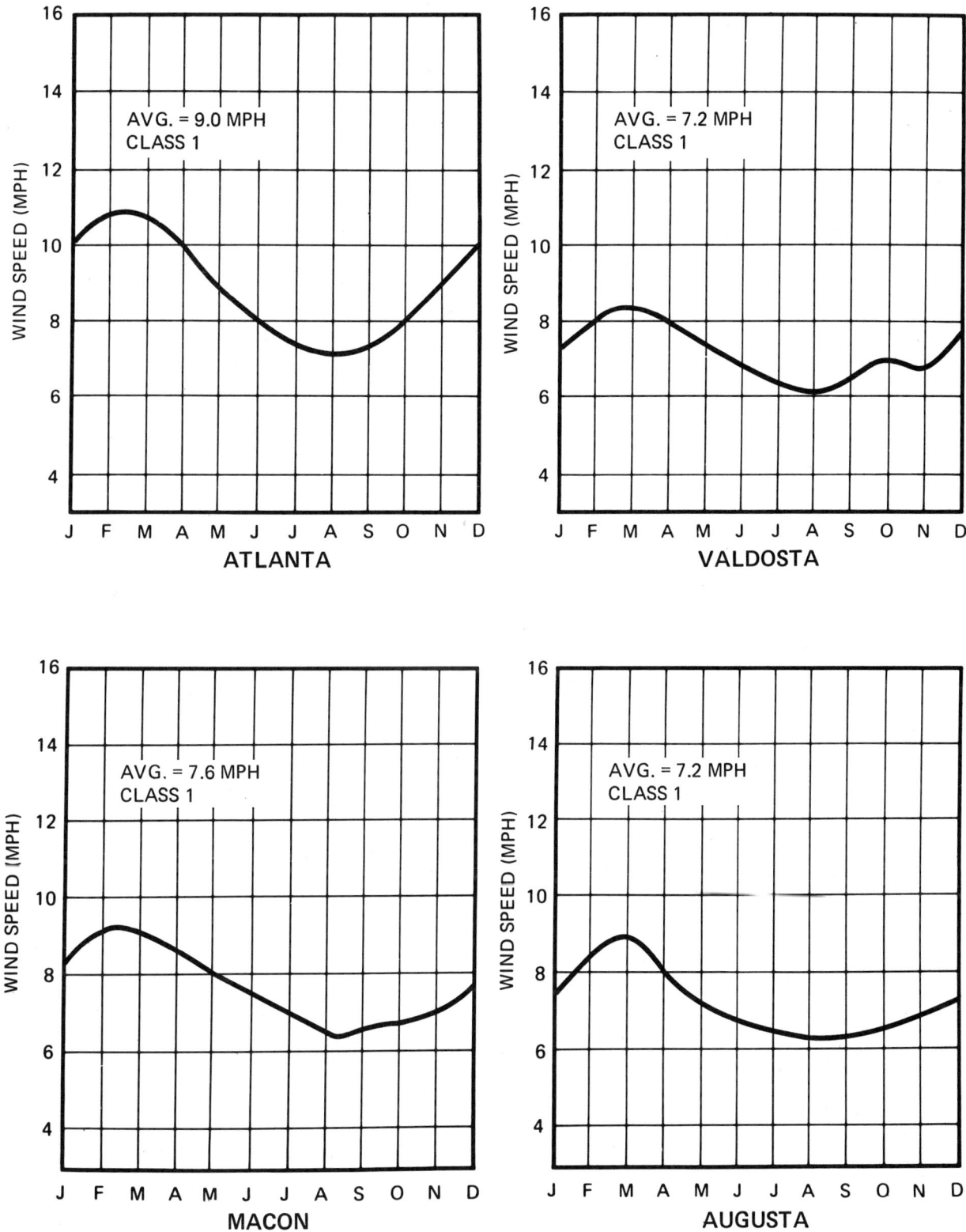

Fig. 65 Monthly average wind speeds in Georgia.

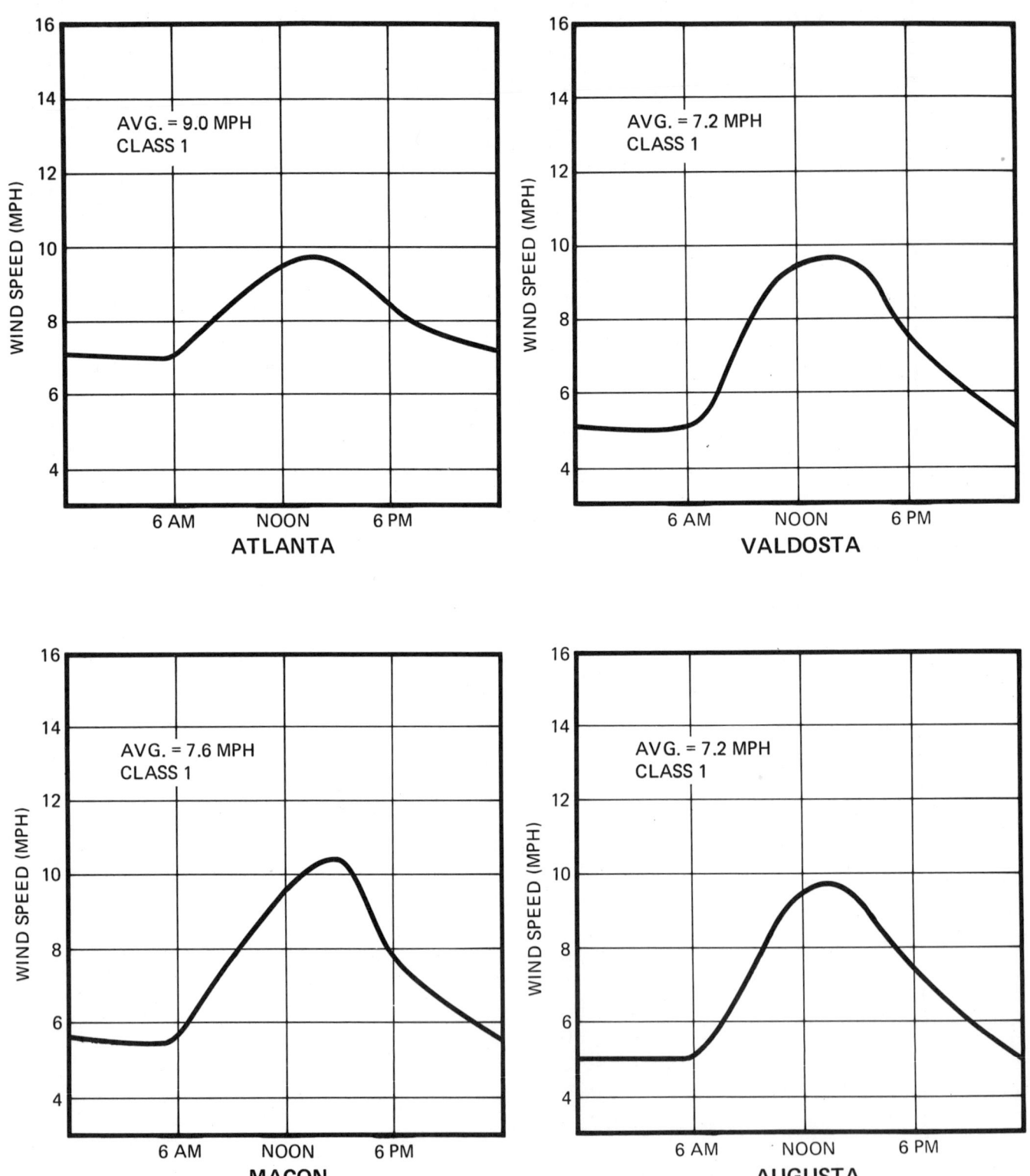

Fig. 66 Hourly average wind speeds in Georgia.

SOUTH CAROLINA

YEARLY AVERAGE WIND SPEEDS

Wind speeds in South Carolina are typical of those in other southeastern states. Some wind machines exist in the small mountainous region in the northwest and along the immediate shore of the Atlantic Ocean and the adjacent islands and peninsulas. The inland plains and rolling hills that comprise most of the territory of South Carolina, however, offer precious few promising sites for economical wind machine operation.

Yearly average wind speeds by wind speed class are shown in Fig. 67. Atop the Blue Ridge that crosses the extreme northwestern part of the state (shaded area in Fig. 67) and that has mountains as high as 3500 ft, winds average Class 3 to Class 4 (11.5 to 13.4 mph). Since even its high ridges are heavily forested, however, the strongest wind speeds are available only in large cleared areas or well above the forest height. The Blue Ridge foothills have Class 2 winds over their tops. On the lower mountain slopes and valleys, winds are usually much less strong.

The shores of the Atlantic, and especially the islands and peninsulas that are exposed to the prevailing southerlies, experience Class 3 winds; well offshore, winds rise to Class 6. Between the mountains and the ocean—or in about 98 percent of the state—winds average Class 1.

SEASONAL AVERAGE WIND SPEEDS

Maps of average wind speeds for the four seasons are shown in Fig. 68 for winter and summer and in Fig. 69 for spring and autumn. Winds are Class 1 during all seasons between the mountains and the sea. Over the narrow foothill and mountain regions, winter is marked by Class 3 (foothill) to Class 6 (mountain crests) winds; in summer, winds are Class 1 over all areas. Coastal winds change less, from Class 2 or Class 3 in winter to Class 1 or Class 2 in summer. As for the transitional seasons, spring is far windier than autumn over the mountain ridges, having Class 4 or Class 5 winds compared to autumn's Class 2 or Class 3.

Average monthly wind speeds at Charleston, Greenville, Myrtle Beach, and Columbia are shown in Fig. 70. Winds at Charleston average about 2 mph higher than those at the other three locations. The strongest winds occur in late winter and early spring and the weakest in late summer and early autumn. The seasonal change at low elevations is small—only 2 to 3 mph—when compared to that over mountain summits or in the northern states.

AVERAGE WIND SPEEDS BY DAY AND NIGHT

The change in wind speed over the 24-hour cycle is shown for Charleston, Greenville, Myrtle Beach, and Columbia in Fig. 71. Afternoon winds exceed late nighttime winds by a wide margin. At Charleston, winds average 6.5 mph late at night and jump to 11.5 mph in the early afternoon. At Myrtle Beach and Columbia, winds at their afternoon peak are about twice as strong as at sunrise. The smallest difference—3.5 mph—occurs at Greenville.

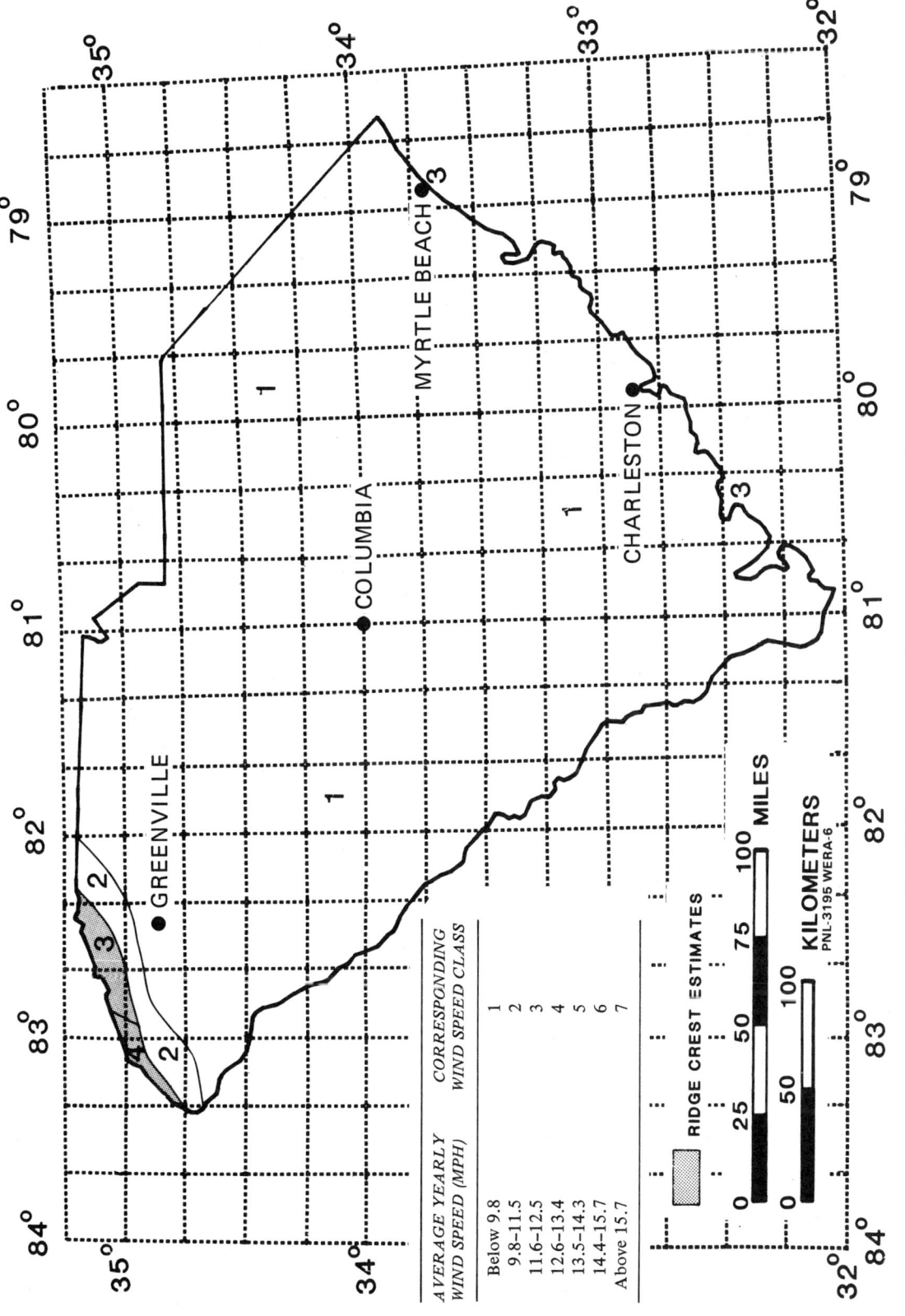

Fig. 67 Yearly average wind speeds in South Carolina.

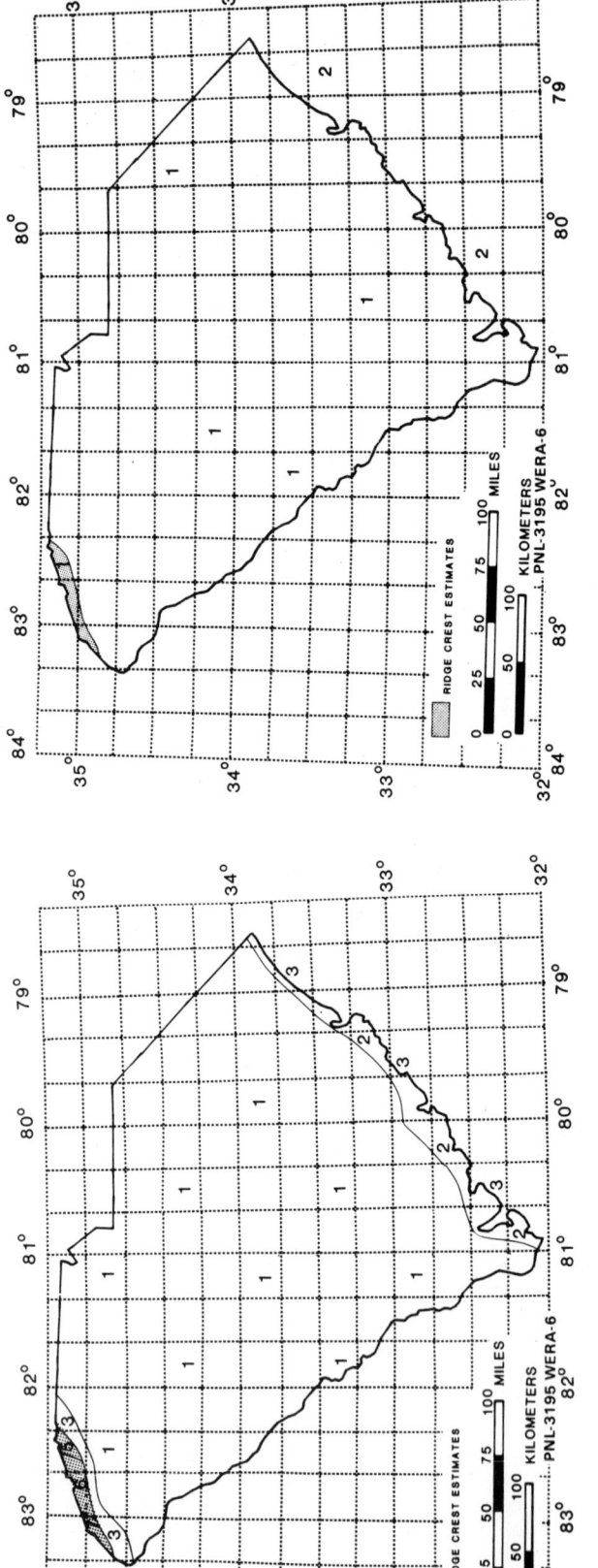

Fig. 68 Seasonal average wind speeds in South Carolina.

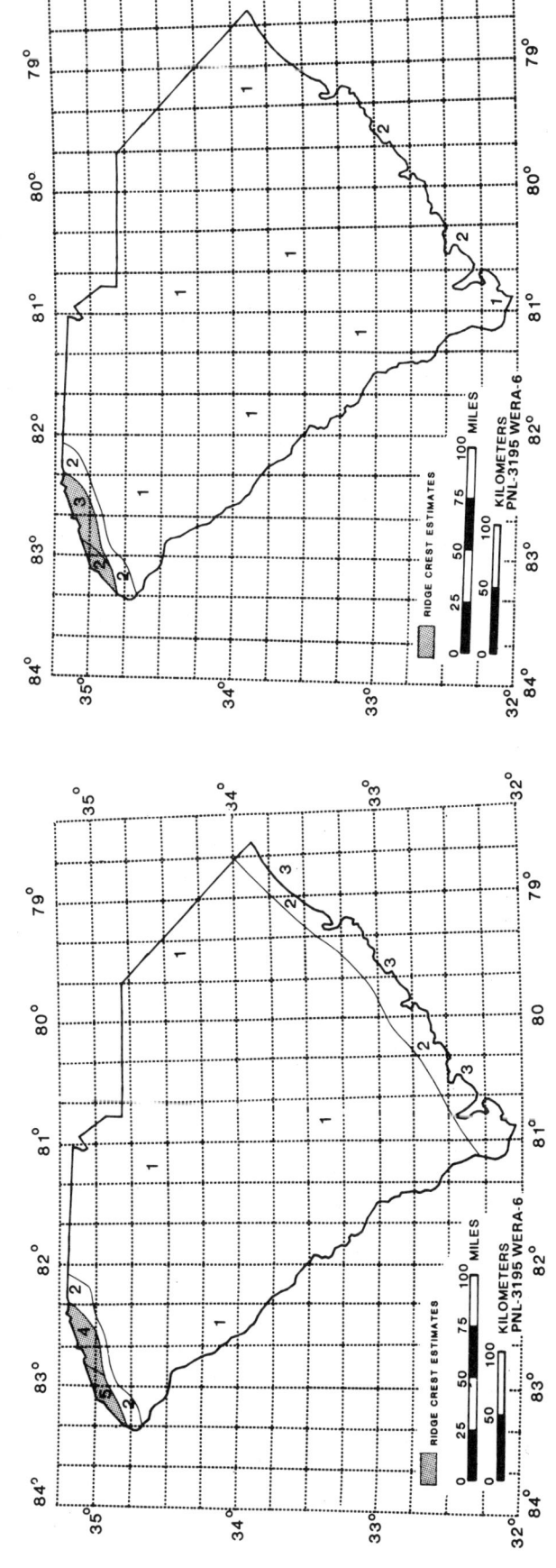

Fig. 69 Seasonal average wind speeds in South Carolina.

SOUTH CAROLINA
MONTHLY AVERAGE WIND SPEED

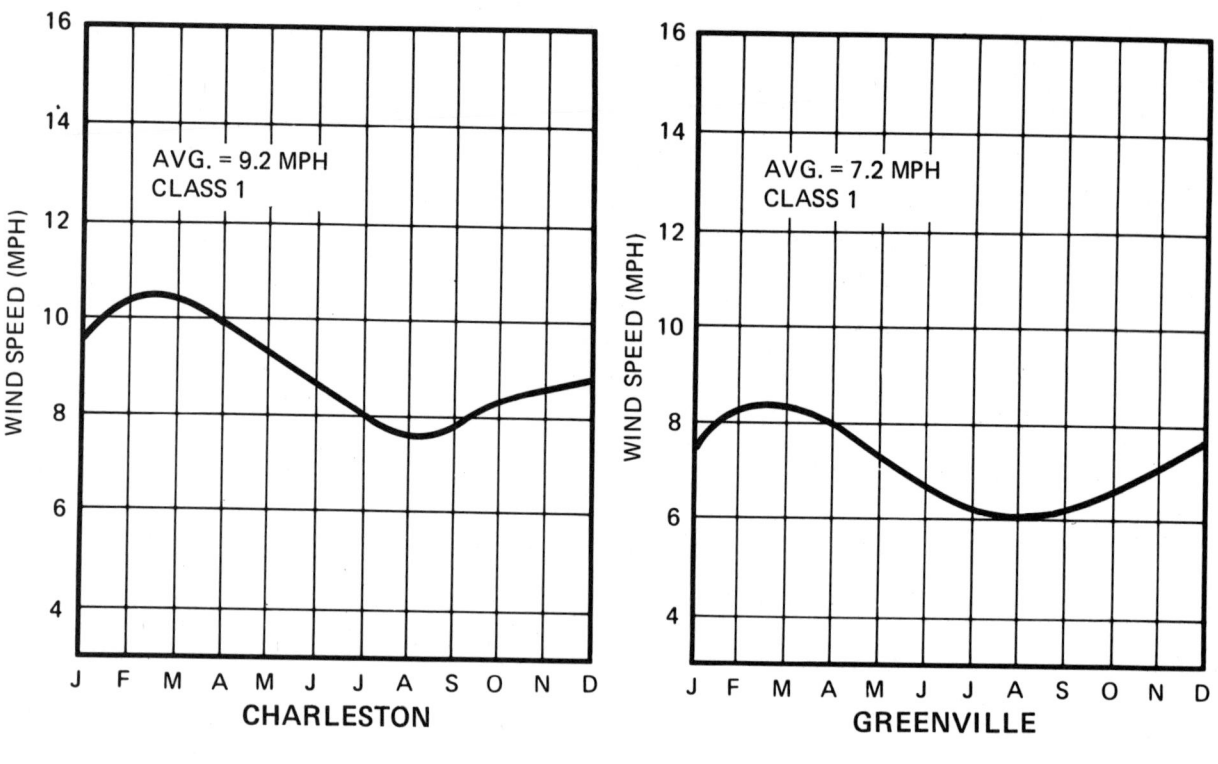

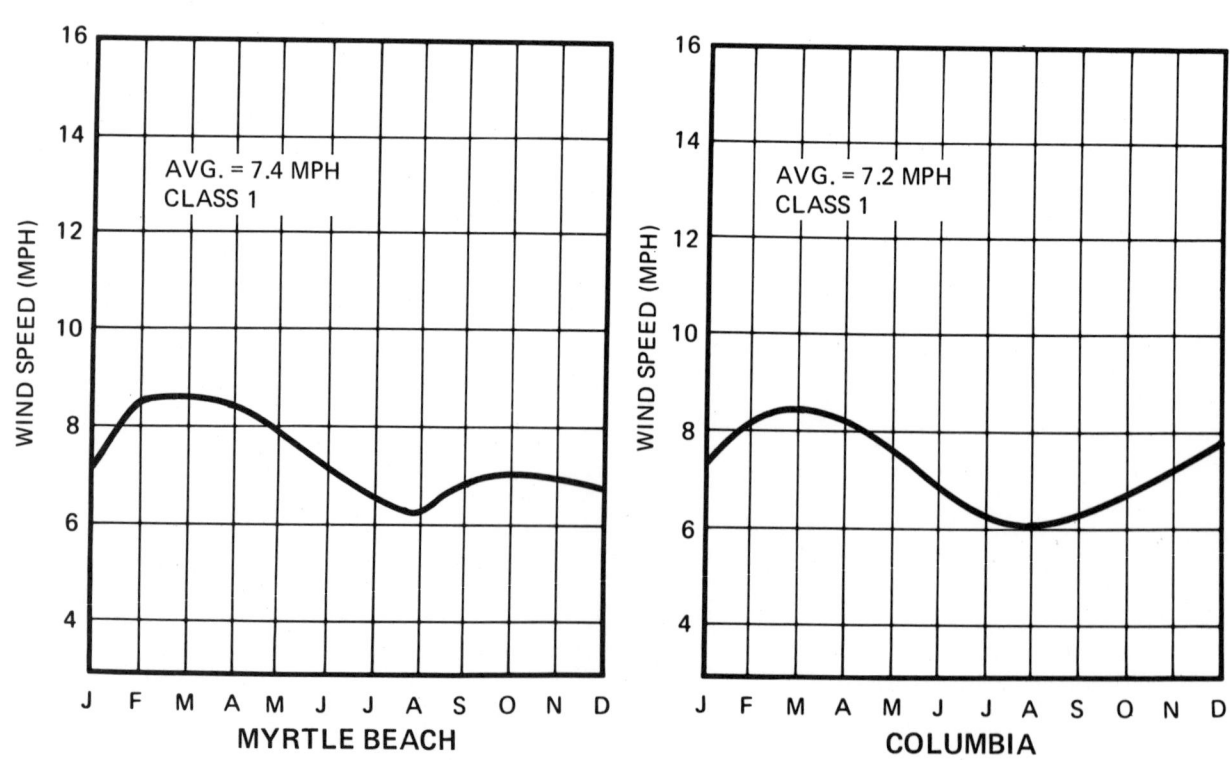

Fig. 70 Monthly average wind speeds in South Carolina.

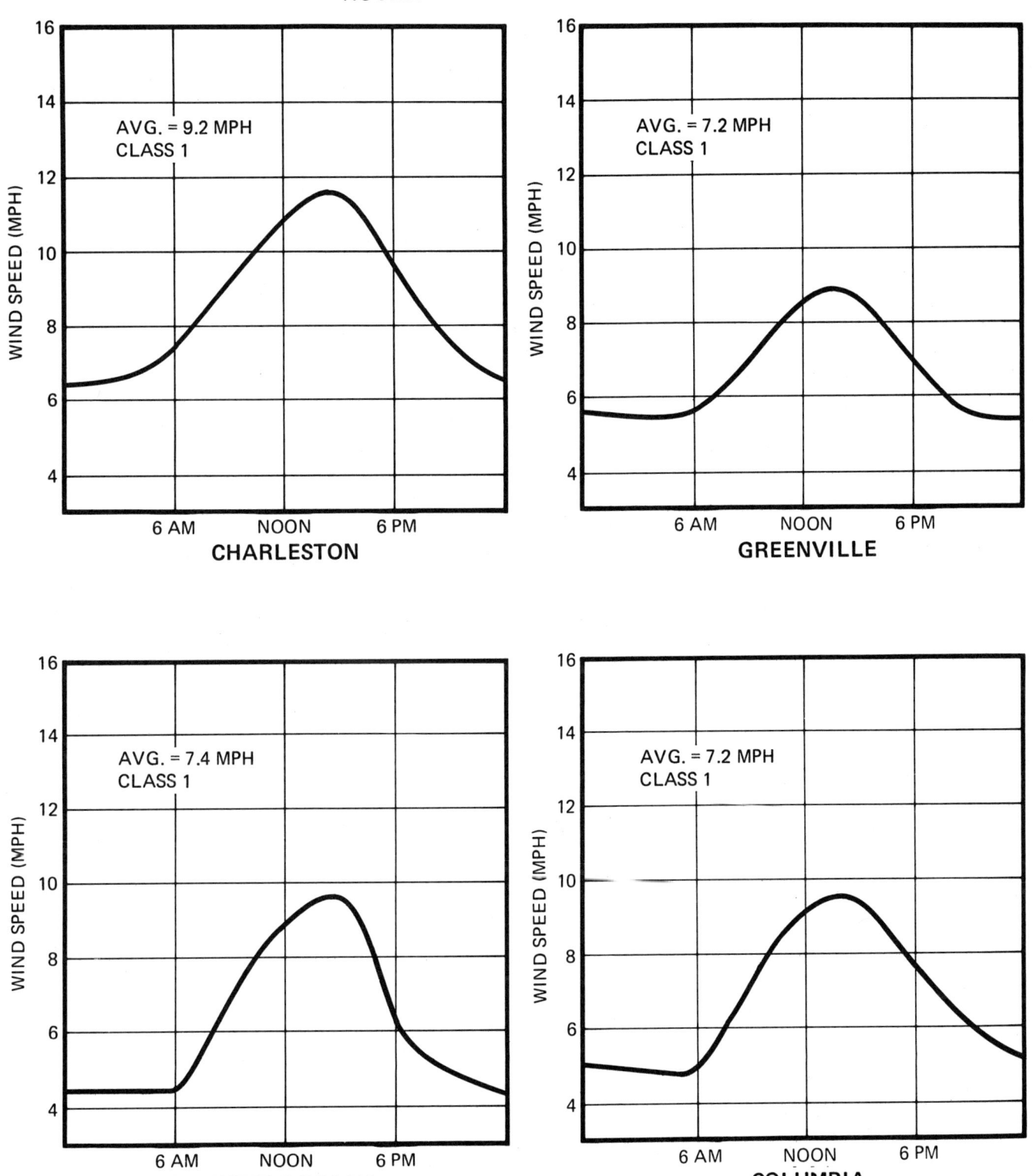

Fig. 71 Hourly average wind speeds in South Carolina.

FLORIDA

YEARLY AVERAGE WIND SPEEDS

Most of Florida has light winds. Only in the coastal regions and islands are they strong enough to consider the use of a wind machine as a means of producing energy less expensive than that obtained from conventional sources.

Yearly average wind speeds in Florida are shown in Fig. 72. In all inland areas, Class 1 winds prevail (less than 9.8 mph) because of the state's low latitude—well south of the storms that regularly pass through the central and northern states. Only trade winds from the southeast through the northeast provide a regular source of airflow. Although the trade winds are steady when compared to the fickle, shifting winds of the storms to the north, they are more inclined to be light or moderate than strong.

The east coast and the Keys average Class 2 or 3 winds, the coastal region experiencing the latter. No more than a very few miles inland, however, winds drop to Class 1. Average wind speeds along Florida's long Gulf of Mexico coastline do not exceed Class 2.

SEASONAL AVERAGE WIND SPEEDS

Average wind speeds change slowly and by a comparatively small amount from season to season. The winds of winter and summer are shown in Fig. 73 and of spring and autumn in Fig. 74. Winds are strongest during winter and spring when speeds average at least Class 2 over the southern half of the state and to a considerable distance inland in the north. During these seasons, Class 3 winds blow over the Keys and along the immediate Atlantic and Gulf coasts.

Summer is a time of light winds; only the Keys and the Atlantic shores afford speeds as high as Class 2. Autumn is scarcely any windier inland, but exposed points on the Atlantic shores experience Class 3 winds.

Monthly average wind speeds at four Florida locations—Panama City (near the Gulf coast in the panhandle), Miami, Orlando, and Key West—are shown in Fig. 75. The strongest winds blow at Panama City in February, and in March or April at the other locations. Late summer is the season of lightest winds. The difference between the windiest and calmest months is 3 to 4 mph. Key West has the strongest winds and Panama City the lightest.

AVERAGE WIND SPEEDS BY DAY AND NIGHT

As in most of the United States, winds in Florida are highest in the afternoon and lightest at night. This pattern is well indicated by Fig. 76, which shows wind speeds at Panama City, Key West, Orlando, and Miami. At Miami, wind speeds double from 6.8 mph at sunrise to over 13 mph at 2 P.M. The difference at Key West, which is surrounded by water, is only 2 mph. Both Keys and peninsulas can be expected to show relatively small differences between day and night wind speeds. Inland, the difference is much greater, particularly during clear weather and in the spring and summer.

112 SOUTH AND SOUTHEAST WIND ATLAS

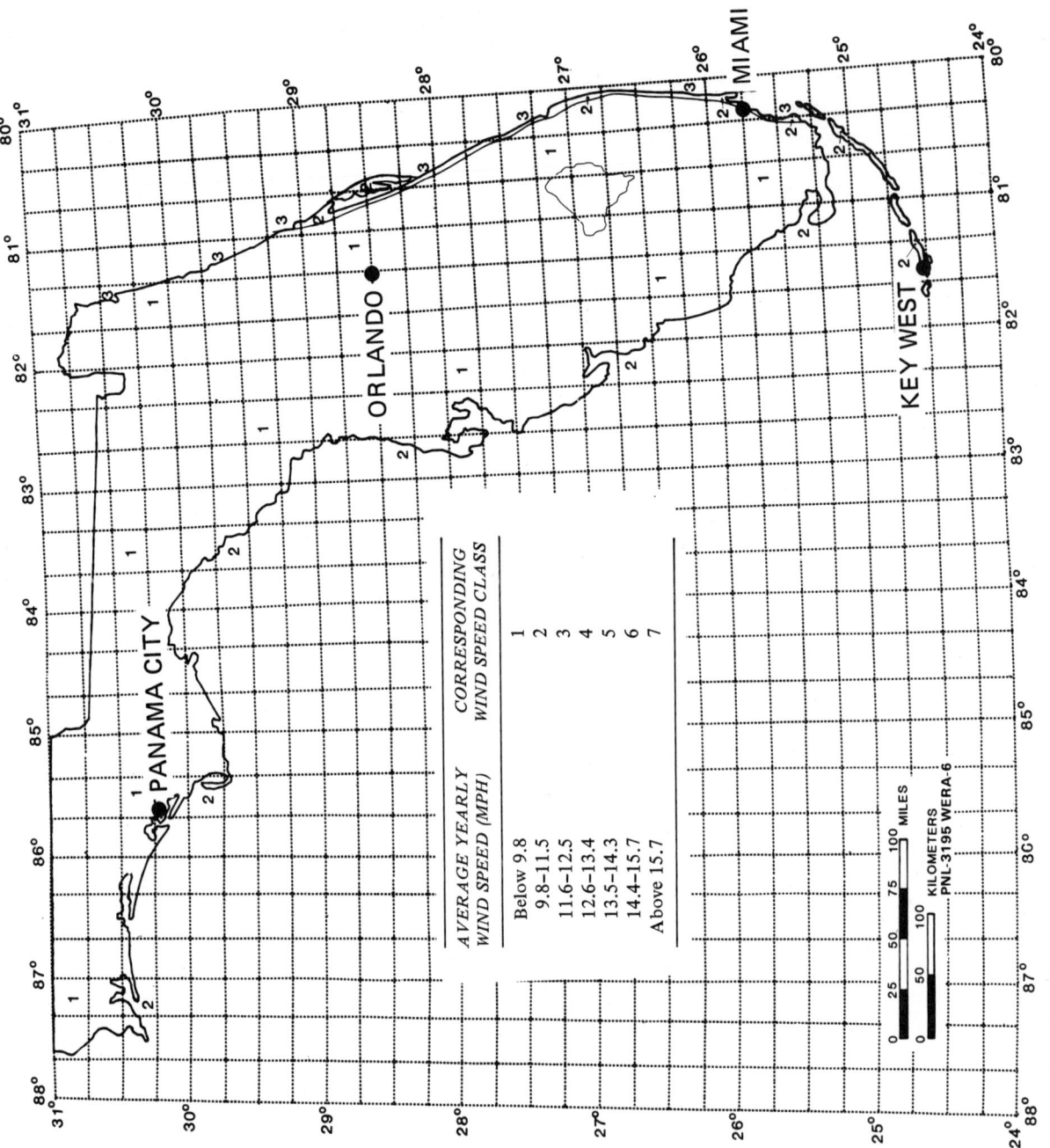

Fig. 72 Yearly average wind speeds in Florida.

FLORIDA 113

AVERAGE YEARLY WIND SPEED (MPH)	CORRESPONDING WIND SPEED CLASS
Below 9.8	1
9.8–11.5	2
11.6–12.5	3
12.6–13.4	4
13.5–14.3	5
14.4–15.7	6
Above 15.7	7

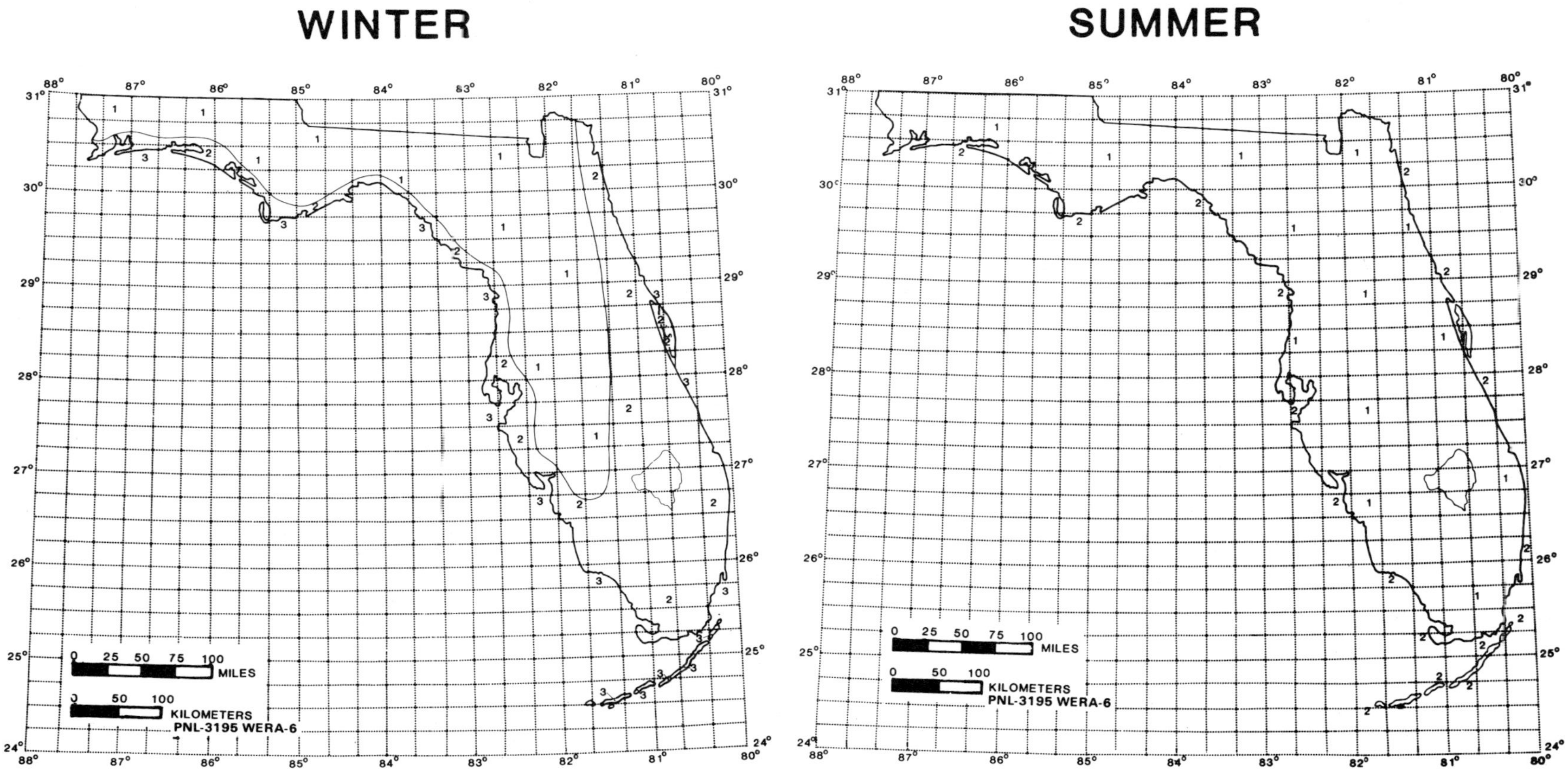

Fig. 73 Seasonal average wind speeds in Florida.

114 SOUTH AND SOUTHEAST WIND ATLAS

AVERAGE YEARLY WIND SPEED (MPH)	CORRESPONDING WIND SPEED CLASS
Below 9.8	1
9.8–11.5	2
11.6–12.5	3
12.6–13.4	4
13.5–14.3	5
14.4–15.7	6
Above 15.7	7

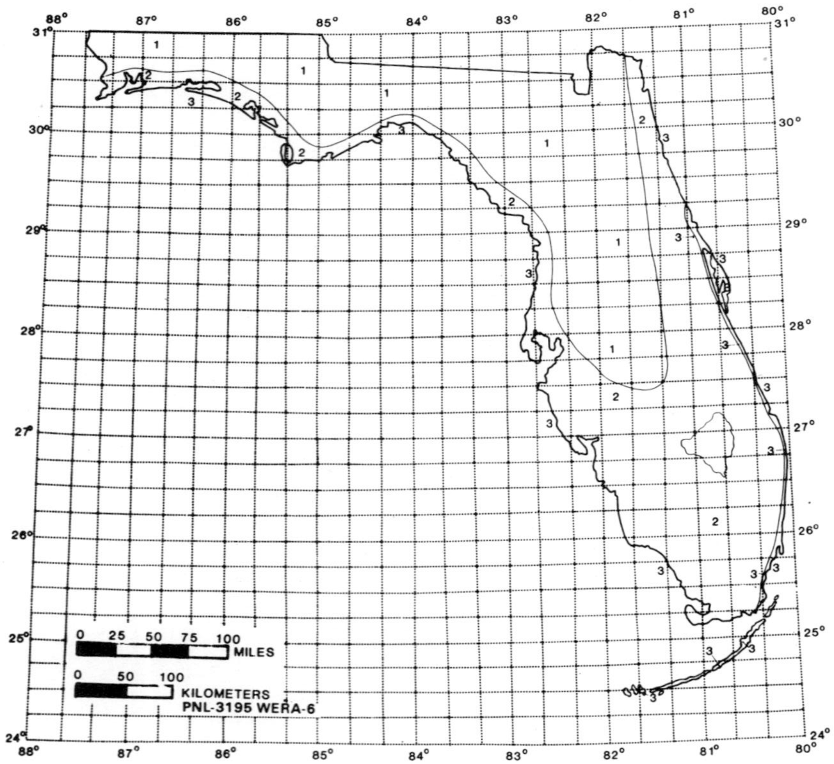

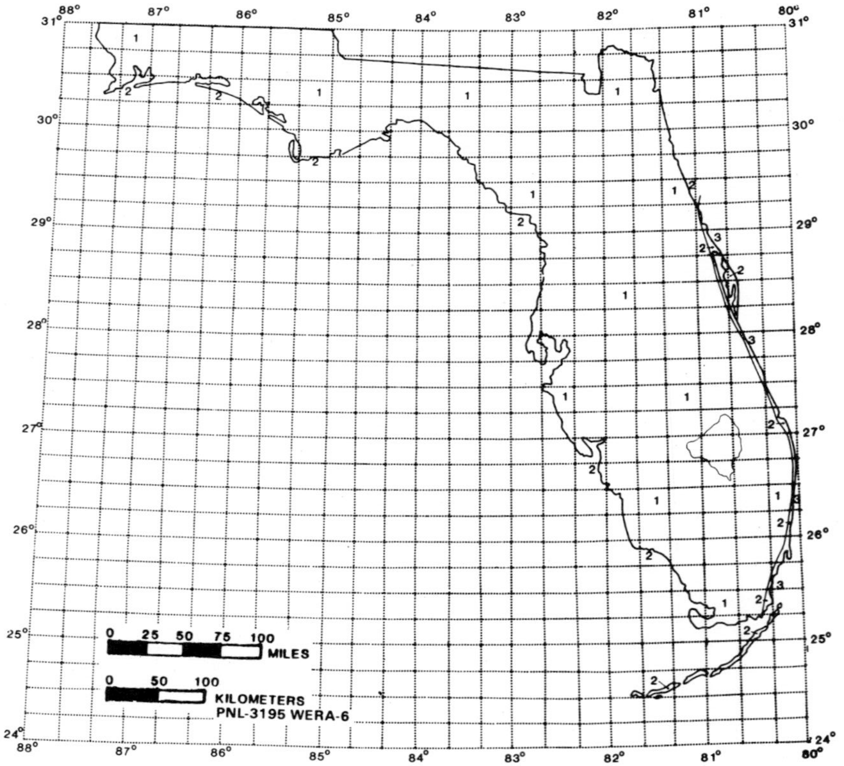

Fig. 74 Seasonal average wind speeds in Florida.

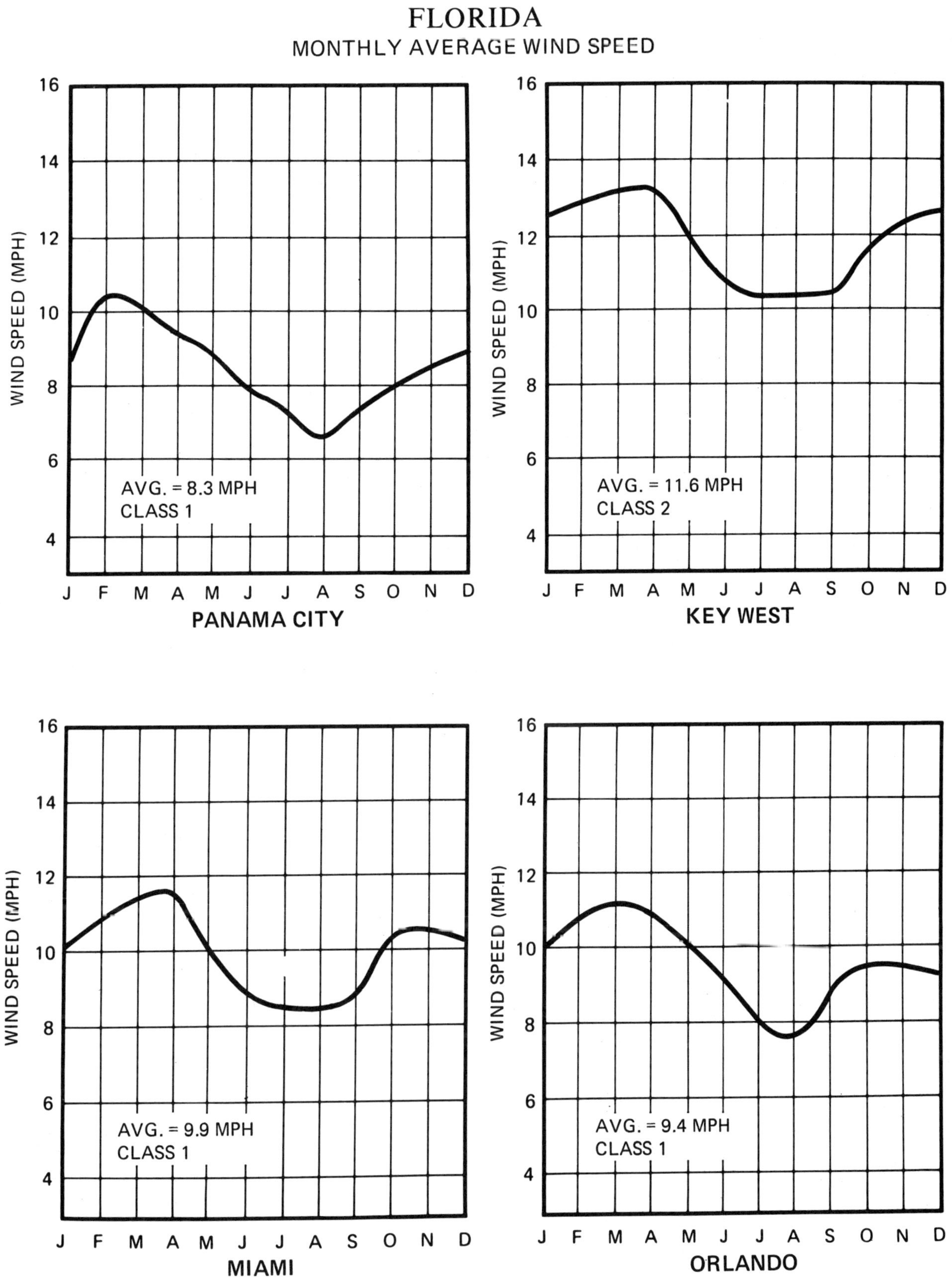
FLORIDA
MONTHLY AVERAGE WIND SPEED
WIND SPEED (MPH)
16
14
12
10
8
6
4
AVG. = 8.3 MPH
CLASS 1
J F M A M J J A S O N D
PANAMA CITY
AVG. = 11.6 MPH
CLASS 2
KEY WEST
AVG. = 9.9 MPH
CLASS 1
MIAMI
AVG. = 9.4 MPH
CLASS 1
ORLANDO

Fig. 75 Monthly average wind speeds in Florida.

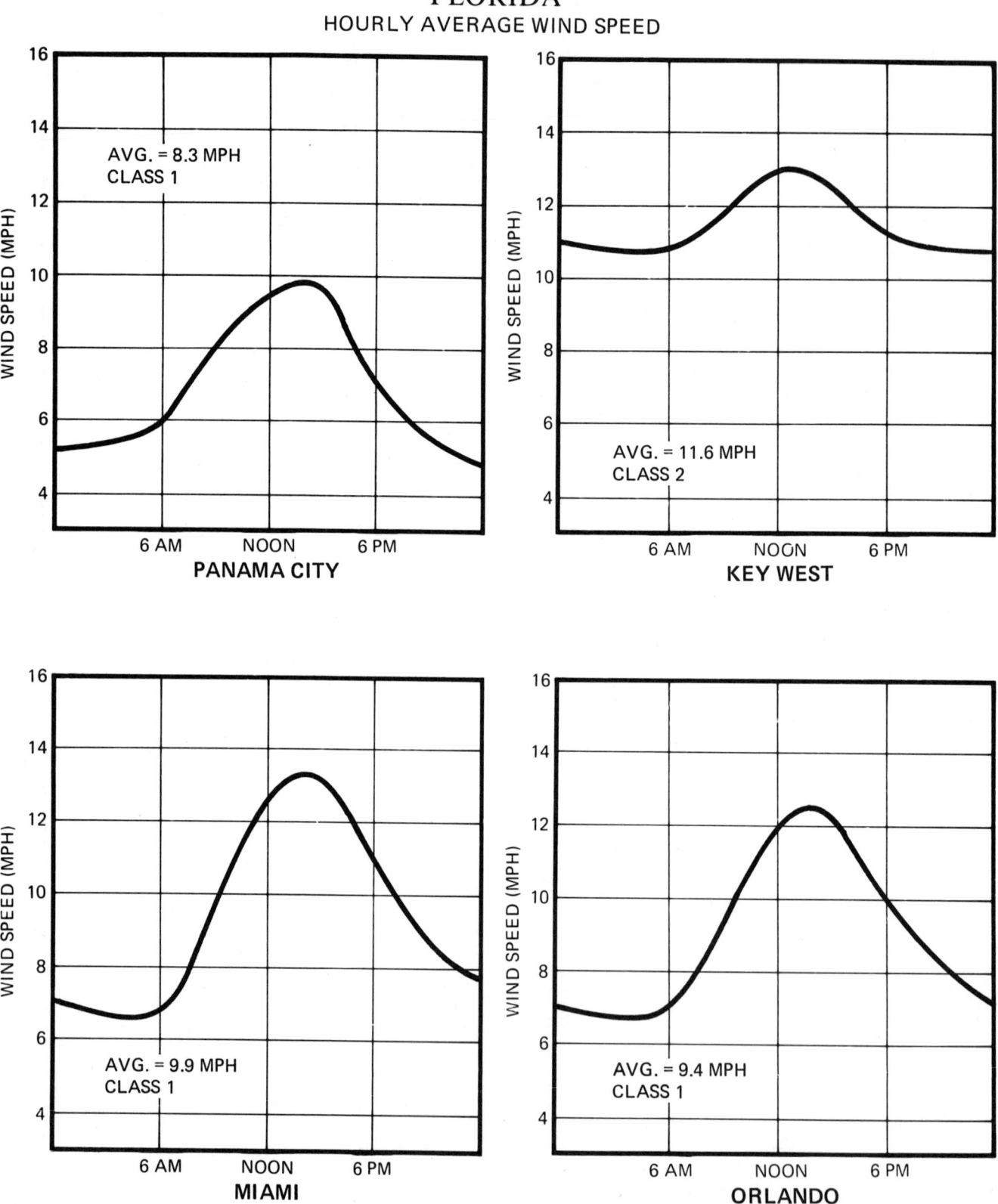

Fig. 76 Hourly average wind speeds in Florida.

WIND SPEED AND WIND POWER AT VARIOUS LOCATIONS IN THE SOUTHEAST REGION

The table that follows shows the yearly average wind speed and the yearly average wind power at each location in the Southeast Region where winds are measured frequently and reliably. Not enough measurements have been made at other locations to provide the basis for computing reliable yearly averages. (For a definition of wind power and its relationship to average wind speed, refer to page 3.)

TOWN, CITY, OR PLACE	FACILITY	YEARLY AVERAGE WIND SPEED (MPH AT 33 FT ABOVE GROUND)	YEARLY AVERAGE WIND POWER (WATTS PER SQ. METER)
MISSISSIPPI			
Biloxi	Biloxi Airport	6.9	70
Columbus	Columbus Air Force Base	5.0	43
Greenville	Greenville Air Force Base	6.7	51
Greenwood	Greenwood Airport	10.1	110
Jackson	A.C. Thompson Field	7.4	67
McComb	McComb Airport	6.7	44
Meridian	Key Field	5.8	42
ALABAMA			
Anniston	Anniston Calhoun County Airport	6.3	45
Birmingham	Birmingham Municipal Airport	6.9	50
Dothan	Dothan Airport	7.6	57
Evergreen	Evergreen Airport	5.6	33
Cairns	Ft. Rucker Field	5.8	37
Huntsville	Huntsville/Madison County Airport	8.3	74
Mobile	Bates Field	9.0	78
Mobile	Brookley Air Force Base	7.4	58
Montgomery	Danelly Field	7.2	50
Muscle Shoals	Muscle Shoals Airport	7.4	57
Selma	Craig Air Force Base	5.8	34
Tuscaloosa	Tuscaloosa Municipal Airport	5.6	33
GEORGIA			
Albany	Albany Naval Air Station	5.2	30
Alma	Bacon County Airport	6.5	45
Athens	Athens Municipal Airport	6.7	51
Atlanta	Hartsfield Airport	9.0	69
Augusta	Bush Field	7.2	51
Brunswick	Glynco Naval Air Station	6.3	41
Columbus	Columbus Municipal Airport	7.2	46
Macon	L.B. Wilson Field	7.6	56
Marietta	Dobbins Air Force Base	5.6	40
Rome	R.B. Russell Field	6.3	40
Savannah	Savannah Municipal Airport	8.1	61

TOWN, CITY, OR PLACE	FACILITY	YEARLY AVERAGE WIND SPEED (MPH AT 33 FT ABOVE GROUND)	YEARLY AVERAGE WIND POWER (WATTS PER SQ. METER)
GEORGIA (continued)			
Valdosta	Valdosta Municipal Airport	7.2	46
Warner Robins	Robins Air Force Base	5.6	42
SOUTH CAROLINA			
Anderson	Anderson County Airport	7.8	68
Beaufort	Marine Corps Air Station	6.3	43
Charleston	Charleston International Airport	9.2	83
Columbia	Columbia Airport	7.2	48
Eastover	McIntire Air National Guard Base	6.0	42
Florence	City-County Airport	8.3	57
Greenville	Greenville-Spartanburg Jet Age Airport	7.2	45
Myrtle Beach	Myrtle Beach Air Force Base	7.4	62
Spartanburg	Downtown Memorial Airport	7.6	60
Sumter	Shaw Air Force Base	6.3	45
FLORIDA			
Avon Park	Avon Park Air Force Base	5.4	31
Cape Kennedy	Cape Kennedy Air Force Base	7.6	52
Cocoa Beach	Patrick Air Force Base	10.1	113
Daytona Beach	Daytona Regional Airport	9.0	83
Ft. Myers	Page Field	8.7	74
Homestead	Homestead Air Force Base	7.8	73
Jacksonville	Jacksonville International Airport	7.6	64
Key West	Key West International Airport	11.6	132
Miami	Miami International Airport	9.9	95
Milton	Whiting Naval Air Station	6.0	40
Orlando	Herndon Field	9.4	84
Panama City	Tyndall Air Force Base	8.3	77
Pensacola	Saufley Field	8.1	72
Tallahassee	Tallahassee Municipal Airport	6.7	43
Tampa	Tampa International Airport	8.7	64
Valparaiso	Eglin Air Force Base	7.4	54
West Palm Beach	Palm Beach International Airport	10.4	112